Forward!

Forward!

Thoughts of a Trans Woman
on the Christian Journey

LYNN ELIZABETH WALKER

Foreword by David E. Weekley

RESOURCE *Publications* · Eugene, Oregon

FORWARD!
Thoughts of a Trans Woman on the Christian Journey

Resource Publications
An Imprint of Wipf and Stock Publishers
199 W. 8th Ave., Suite 3
Eugene, OR 97401

www.wipfandstock.com

PAPERBACK ISBN: 978-1-6667-6280-8
HARDCOVER ISBN: 978-1-6667-6281-5
EBOOK ISBN: 978-1-6667-6282-2

VERSION NUMBER 071923

The New Revised Standard Version is used for all scriptural references. Fewer than 500 verses have been quoted. In some instances, the text was revised slightly to ensure clear gender equity.

In memory of DW, my mother,
and in gratitude for my family

Contents

Foreword

David E. Weekley

ALTERITY. I WAS INTRODUCED to this term in *Forward! Thoughts of a Trans Woman on the Christian Journey*, by the Right Reverend Dr. Lynn Elizabeth Walker, who currently serves as the Orthodox Catholic Church's bishop in New York. I met Lynn at the Philadelphia Transgender Health Conference in 2009. We met there with a group of other transgender faith leaders. Many of us were there for the first time and had never met before that conference. I had the opportunity to have a conversation with the bishop, and together we shared our then current ministries and future hopes. As we talked together it was clear she shared a deep passion for ministry among marginalized people—people alienated from community. That was thirteen years ago and since then, each person I met there has continued their unique spiritual journey, as we all do whether we are aware of it or not. It is an honor for me to write this foreword to the faith journey and conversation to which she invites us.

Forward! Thoughts of a Trans Woman on the Christian Journey introduces and exposes the reader to the experience of alterity, the experience of being different, set-aside, viewed, and valued as "less than" other kinds of human beings. Alterity is to be the "other." It is one premise of this book that transgender people organically relate to this experience and are able to communicate and articulate what at heart is a very basic human experience of longing: the longing for the unseen, uncertain future. Bishop Walker points out that sometimes this longing leads people away from God and that one common result of such turning away is to isolate God from our feelings, and then blame God for feeling isolated, ultimately concluding that religion is irrelevant, when the very opposite is true: religion is at the heart of human life. This text calls all people to closely examine this feeling of otherness. She suggests that one possible and significant result of turning back toward God through such an evaluation is a profoundly deep historical and contemporary solidarity with spiritually, politically, and socially marginalized people. Two other invaluable outcomes of such an examination are discussed throughout the book: (1) to regain a right relationship with God and with all people; and (2) to reach out to others and empower them, and in so doing perhaps discover a common connecting thread. Lynn suggests this is a higher power that will lead us forward as we choose to follow.

With clear historical, scriptural, and personal notations, she invites the reader to imagine what to some may seem unimaginable—to consider the experience of being different, of being set-aside and devalued by others. Walker invites cisgender readers to imagine what it is like to be transgender, and asks the question, "Is it really all that different?" To accept the invitation to "come out," whatever that means, allows the reader to enter into a persuasive theological conversation about the very nature of the concept of "difference" itself. For example, in chapter 14, Walker discusses a precept frequently attributed to English Franciscan friar William of Ockham (ca. 1287–1347), a scientist, philosopher, and theologian. The term is known as "Ockham's razor" and proposes that when presented with competing proposals about the same prediction, the solution with the fewest assumptions, and the least complex hypothesis, should be selected. Beyond science and theology, Ockham invited people to ponder the reality of all the complex categories created by the human mind.

Earlier in the text, Walker explored the question of "differences" though a theological framework. Drawing upon Ockham's razor, and turning to the third chapter of Genesis and the topic of disobedience, she asks, "From where or what did disobedience originate?" The answer provided is noteworthy, as it is an important connecting thread in this conversation.

Jesus advised us to be like little children and one of the characteristics of children is simplicity. They have the good sense to avoid trying to separate the parts of their lives into boxes. For them, church, school, and play are all similar, with many of the same people and many of the same rules. In the third chapter of Genesis, the chronicler relates that it was at the moment of disobedience that adults lost the childlike understanding that all things and all places and all situations are fundamentally, profoundly alike. It was as the moment of turning from God that we adults began to use our new wisdom to make distinctions and divisions. Rather than follow God's leadership, we adults develop complex categories and special rules for special situations.

Weaving together personal story and tracing theological history, Walker ultimately returns to the essential human choice presented at the beginning of the book and developed throughout this empowering spiritual memoir. The choice is to choose a right relationship with God and others or turn away. She emphasizes that at this crossroad in human history, reunification and rededication to God through Jesus Christ is a healthy and freeing choice. Affirming Jesus as a living example of the great commandment to love God with all our heart, soul, mind, and strength, and our neighbor as ourselves, is the path of spiritual freedom and flourishing human community. The LGBTQIA+ community, spiritual seekers from all backgrounds, Christian faith leaders, and anyone who accepts the invitation to the journey will find this an inspiring, inviting, challenging, and a hopeful read. I hope you enjoyed the conversation and the trip as much as I did!

Introduction

THERE HAVE BEEN MANY memoirs and autobiographies of trans people over the past three or four decades, as well as useful and interesting discussions of the trans experience from political, social, and many other different perspectives. Perhaps this little book will serve as a useful addition to the conversations. Perhaps these reflections will suggest that much of the application of Christian thought to the trans experience is neither revolutionary nor surprising. Rather, it might be said that within the Christian worldview articulated here, the trans experience is much like other experiences in that it is a journey marked by challenges, joys, hardships, frustrations, lessons, and victories. It is also a journey that is enriched through the experience of prayer and spirituality.

This collection is rooted in numerous experiences over three decades, especially in support groups at the Gender Identity Project within the LGBT Community Center in New York City, conversations and worship at Dignity NYC, conversations with the late Dr. Leo Wollman, collaborative work with the International Foundation for Gender Education, and a number of local gatherings in New York.

Too many to name are the people whose friendship, intelligence, initiative, grace, humor, and insights have exerted a significant influence. Profound thanks are due to all of them, and to countless others, without whose encouragement this work might not have been completed.

1

Alterity: The Sense of Being Different

HAVE YOU EVER GONE to a foreign country where they speak a different language? That happened to me in Texas (where they speak Texan) but also, more seriously, and more recently, in Panama. I honestly have almost no useful understanding of the Spanish language, though I can sometimes get the sense of street signs and menus if the words are close enough to French or Latin. I was lost. How must it have felt, I sometimes wonder, for my great grandparents, landing on Ellis Island knowing only German. Going from there to Brooklyn where only a few people spoke German and trying to learn this new English language while also trying to earn a living and raise a family. Uncomfortable in the extreme, but it could be worse: have you heard of people going to a place where the folks understood English but refused to use it to communicate with the American tourists? Heap frustration upon frustration, add insult to injury. It happens.

The Egyptian Thebaid—the desert to which the first monastics fled for solitude—was not exactly a hospitable place. At best it was neutral; occasionally it was a howling wasteland. Yet, in the very early years of the Common Era, it was the birthplace of Christian monasticism. Isolated from others, seekers and mystics, visionaries and lunatics fled to the desert to be alone with themselves, seeking

God. "O God you are my God, I seek you, my soul thirsts for you, my flesh faints for you, as in a dry and weary land where there is no water" (Ps 63:1). And then came pilgrims, visitors, and other various followers, seekers, and gadflies. And quasi communities of hermits, anchorites, and solitaries began to grow. There, language and common life were secondary to the movement of the spirit and the striving of the individual soul for salvation. An individual might spend years, even an entire lifetime, in holy solitude. For the Desert Fathers and Desert Mothers, life was always to be a stranger in a strange land, a pilgrim passing through.

Similar, no doubt, was the experience of so many other wanderers and travelers. Abraham, particularly, found himself a stranger upon his departure from Ur, to wander according to the command of the Lord. Moses, still in Egypt, named his son Gershom, for he said he had been a stranger in strange land, echoing the words of the Lord to Abraham in sleep. And of course, the people of Israel during the many years of wandering from Egypt to Canaan. For so many people in this century, it is not uncommon to move many times in the course of a lifetime and there is a consequent sense of rootlessness and restlessness that gnaws at the corners of our minds.

If you do not know where you are going, how will you know when you have arrived? Sir John de Mandeville, a medieval Englishman, wrote one of the first narratives of traveling, in French, in the 1350s. Very popular, the work was translated into Latin and English, and describes in great detail the marvels he had seen in the Holy Land, and in Asia and the lands beyond India. Readers loved this, not only for its usefulness, but for its strangeness. Useful, you see, because if you are going on pilgrimage to Jerusalem, you want to know what it is like before you get there. Otherwise, how will you know when you have arrived? On the other hand, is it not wonderful and fascinating to know that in the middle part of India, which you are unlikely ever to visit for any reason, there are folk who have only one foot, and it is so large that they can use it to shield themselves from the heat of the sun while they rest?

For some of the same reasons do people even now go down to the boardwalk in Coney Island to see the amazing bearded lady, the elastic man, the fire-eater, and the world's largest canary. And they go to the Bronx Zoo to see aardvarks, otters, and zebras; and lions and tigers and bears. And they come to Greenwich Village to see fags, dykes, and drag folk. And trans folk, leather people, and any other kind of visibly recognizable queer. See, there are at least two sides to this business of being a stranger in a strange land. One is, of course, the experience of alienation and alterity experienced by the object of observation, and the other is the fascination, interest, or even repulsion, fear, or disgust experienced by the observer.

And it is not just a matter of culture, language, and linguistics. A couple of years ago, the very useful point was made that similar communication difficulties arise even within the English language: do you remember the books by Deborah Tannen a couple of years ago? For that matter, do you remember *Alice's Adventures in Wonderland* and *Through the Looking-Glass*? Does it not sometimes seem as if the people all round us are from another planet? We trans folk have certainly had the experience for so very many years of being utterly unable to communicate effectively with those who do not share much of our experience. How on earth can we possibly have a coherent conversation about this most important aspect of our lives, or about any aspect of our lives that may be touched by the fact of our trans identity, when the person listening has not even the first idea of what we are talking about? They can no more understand us than we can understand them. Do you ever wonder what it must be like to be non-transgender? Is it really that much different, do you think?

To be a stranger is to know alienation, to know isolation, to know the ghetto. To be a stranger is to be directed with Rosa Parks to the back of the bus, to be imprisoned with Nelson Mandela, It is to be a thing observed by others. It is to be less than real, less than legitimate, less than worthy, less than human. It has nearly nothing to do with majority or minority status in any terms whatsoever, as we have seen in Rhodesia, in Ireland, in South Africa, and in North America. It has everything to do with guile, power and

3

control, and oppression. It has to do with personal, visceral hatred and not with mere theoretical or political differences.

The Israelites knew well the taste of oppression during their sojourns in Egypt and Babylon, and later Jews in medieval Europe. The Psalmist lamented, "More in number than the hairs of my head are those that hate me without cause; many are those who would destroy me, my enemies who accuse me falsely" (Ps 69:4). And trans folk know it too, for we know all the flavors of hate crimes, of murders and assaults and queer baiting and queer bashing, of suicides and rejection by family and friends, and transphobia even within our own community, and widespread homophobia and disinformation perpetrated by the hypocrites of the so-called "Christian right" who like to talk so blandly about "loving the sinner and hating the sin" and the various right-wing militias and political action groups.

To be a stranger is to know a peculiar kind of longing, for something unseen but somehow known, perhaps dimly remembered, or envisioned through the stories of others. "As the deer longs for flowing streams, so longs my soul for you, O God. My soul thirsts for God, for the living God. When shall I come and behold the face of God?" (Ps 42:1–2). Sometimes we may see only dimly, as in a mirror, or even not at all, but there is still that nagging, driving, unrelenting sense of longing. There is that intuition that there is, that there must be, the object of our desire.

My other great grandfather returned to his ancestral home in Glasgow from Brooklyn many times, and told his mother and sisters about America, where he was no longer a school teacher (as he had been in Scotland) but a steamfitter. And in their longing for a new life in a new land where things just had to better, in their longing for this unknown future, in their longing for a kind of completion in their lives, they left family, friends, and parish and went with him to America. Stepping out of familiar surroundings, stepping away from the only world they had ever known, they took what might be poetically termed a "leap of faith," and their world, their lives, changed forever.

Like my great grandfather, we are all longing for the unseen, for the uncertain future. In the Middle Ages, and throughout many centuries, it was and has been the common dream of many to go on a pilgrimage to Rome, Jerusalem, or Canterbury, or more recently Beaupré or Lourdes: mythic places shrouded in the mists of legend and described so wondrously by Geoffrey Chaucer, Sir John de Mandeville, and others. As the Psalmist sang, "My soul longs, indeed it faints, for the courts of the Lord" (Ps 84:2). Many left to go on pilgrimage and some returned home while others died enroute or stayed.

We are longing for the unknown. So many of us, on the verge of "going public" with family and friends, on the verge perhaps of transition, cannot but wonder just exactly what, in the name of all that is holy, we are doing. It seems like a good thing, it seems like Jerusalem, it seems like it is exactly what we want. But what do any of us know? Will our lives be better, really? What real certainty can we have, aside from what we believe to be the sincere testimony of other pilgrims, other wanderers? But is it not this way with all transitions, all life changes, all movements from mere stasis? Entering a monastery, getting married, celebrating birth, or mourning the loss of a family member all involve a certain amount of change, a certain amount of moving forward into the unknown. We enter into the unknown every day; the degree of intensity and the longing may vary considerably from day to day, from moment to moment, from event to event, but still, we begin each day with only the merest apprehension of what might be in store for us.

To be a stranger is simply to be there, without any history. The priest Melchizedek, the king of Salem who offered bread and wine in thanksgiving to God on behalf of Abraham, seemed to have had no forbears, no family, no one from whom he inherited his priesthood or his personhood (Gen 14:17–20). Many centuries later John the Forerunner was asked, "Who are you?" and he answered by negatives: "I am not the Messiah," not Elijah, and not the prophet, and he finally said, "I am the voice of one crying in the wilderness" (John 1:19–23). Nothing here about his having parents or family. Like Melchizedek, John simply is. Jesus, too, was faced by a hostile crowd to whom he said, "You know neither me nor my Father. If you knew me, you would know my Father also" (John 8:19b). If John is the voice, and Jesus is the Word, the Word is truth, and it is the Word heralded by the voice of John.

Many of us seem to be, as it were, born anew, as if from the very air, or from ourselves, in our fourth, fifth, or sixth decade of life. Our own parents would not know us, nor would our families, friends, and neighbors. We seem to be simply here. Jesus is said to have remarked, "Who is my mother and who are my brothers? Whoever does the will of my Father in heaven" (Matt 12:48b, 50). It is in seeking to know God's will for us as people of transgender experience and in seeking the strength to carry it out, that so often we find ourselves entirely alone, forsaken, and cut off from our own histories. It is in that stark aloneness that we may approach closer to God, to other trans folk, and to ourselves. In that barrenness, that aridity, we may finally find time for ourselves and for our quest for self-definition.

To be a stranger is to come out. In about his thirtieth year, Jesus the carpenter came from Nazareth of Galilee and was baptized by John in the Jordan. And after John was arrested, Jesus came into Galilee, preaching the gospel of God and saying, "The time is fulfilled, and the kingdom of God has come near; return and believe in the good news" (Mark 1:15). Responding to a call or to a heartfelt need, and "coming out" with opinions, feelings, and honesty, is rarely easy, and it is not always welcomed by family, friends, neighbors, and coworkers. Too often, it results in crucifixion and obscurity. Only a few martyrs are remembered.

Yet, to emerge from the closet as trans into the wide world is finally to take a deep breath of freedom. It is to come out as a debutante comes out: into a group of people, a community of similar experience with similar goals, interests, and expectations, who know well the sense of alienation and isolation, who know well the sense of longing which has no words, and who will walk part of the way with us. It is to have incredible confidence in and longing for the future, as well as to have unquenchable optimism.

And sometimes, it is simply to have unspeakable desperation and hunger, and nothing left to lose.

In the ninth chapter of his gospel, St. Luke recounts that Jesus said, "The Son of Man must undergo great suffering, and be rejected by the elders, chief priests, and scribes, and be killed" (Luke 9:21), and then he went on to say, "If any want to become my followers, let them deny themselves and take up their cross daily and follow me. For those who want to save their life will lose it, and those who lose their life for my sake will save it" (Luke 9:23–24). The Christ not only had a pretty good understanding of his own experience of rejection, but also knew what a fine mess his followers were getting themselves into by following him. It did not seem to have taken a long time for the initial euphoria to wear off and for the crowd to decide that he was too radical or not radical enough, that he was too frivolous or too holy, that he talked too much or healed too many, or paid scant attention to the laws of Moses. In his eleventh chapter, St. Matthew records that Jesus said, "But to what shall I compare this generation? It is like children sitting in the market places and calling to one another, 'We piped the flute for you, and you did not dance; we wailed, and you did not mourn.' For John came neither eating nor drinking, and they say, 'He has a demon'; the son of man came eating and drinking, and they say, 'Behold, a glutton and a drunkard, a friend of tax collectors and sinners!'" (Matt 11:16–19).

And still, he loved them. His lament for Jerusalem echoes the grief of David on the death of Absalom: "Jerusalem, Jerusalem, the city that kills the prophets and stones those who are sent to it! How often I have desired to gather your children together as a hen gathers her brood under her wings, and you were not willing!" (Matt 23:37). So much of the pain of alienation comes from this sense that love is rejected, that selfhood is rejected, that identity is rejected, that honest efforts to build bridges are not only rejected but sabotaged, that the meanings of words and thoughts are twisted and misinterpreted and rendered into something else. Rejection is not neutral, it is not merely theoretical. Even rejection and oppression that grows from political exigencies are still personal and painful.

Still, Jesus takes even this and calls it holy: "Blessed are those who are persecuted for righteousness' sake, for theirs is the kingdom of heaven. Blessed are you when people revile you and persecute you and utter all kinds of evil against you falsely on my account. Rejoice and be glad, for your reward is great in heaven, for so people persecuted the prophets who were before you" (Matt 5:10–12). And later in the same chapter Jesus continues: "Love your enemies and pray for those who persecute you" (Matt 5:44b). There is that reference to the "kingdom of heaven" again. It seems that there is something here between the lines, almost as if life itself has a different meaning from its own events and incidents. Almost as if there is an obscure meta text that has yet to be fully explicated, but which is the key to the beginning of full understanding.

There are always multiple levels of meaning in a text, and our very lives are narrative texts with many levels and shades of meanings. It is up to us to step back, as it were, from our lives and begin to see them as life stories, so that we may more easily begin to analyze and meditate upon them, looking for patterns, cycles, and recurring themes.

In finding cycles and patterns, in finding the narrative texts in our lives, we extract power from the very stuff of our lives, and we discover, perhaps, the hand of a higher power leading and guiding us.

We are called to look deeply and long into our feelings of isolation, of alienation, and of alterity or otherness—even into our despair and suicidal depressions—so that we might discover therein the strength and courage to define and crystallize those feelings and sensations. For by doing that work, we will be able to reach out to others who are similarly beset by these same feelings: fellow travelers, fellow pilgrims, seekers, visionaries, and mystics who all share our pain, our loss, and our longing. And in reaching out, in connecting with others, we are strengthened and inspired, and empowered to go on to tomorrow.

There is a fundamental quality of aloneness in each of our lives. The ancient Job observed that naked (and alone, generally) do we come into this world, and naked (and alone, generally) do we die (Job 1:21). Birth and death are supremely individual experiences, yet, indeed, all of life is individual and personal, and all we can really know is our own experience.

The patterns of our lives as trans folk suggests that we may be more acutely aware of this theme in our lives than will non-trans people. And so there are at least two ways to respond. One is to regret or deny the experience, while the other is to make something of it. We are called to make something of our lives and our experiences. We are called to empower ourselves and others, and to demonstrate by our lives that life is fundamentally good, and that the ground of our being is one of strength, love, and power.

2

Bondage (Galatians 3:28)

I LOVE COMING OUT stories. Do you remember the story in the fourth chapter of St. Luke's Gospel about Jesus coming out at the synagogue in his home town of Nazareth? He has been out of town for a while, doing the "Messiah, Child of God" thing, and having returned for a visit, he stood to read the portion from the scripture, as was his custom. It is the part in chapter 61 of the book of the prophet Isaiah that says, "The Spirit of the Lord is upon me, because He has anointed me to preach good news to the poor. He has sent me to proclaim release to the captives and recovery of sight to the blind, to let the oppressed go free, to proclaim the year of the Lord's favor" (Luke 4:18–19). When he has finished, and they are waiting for Jesus's commentary, he sits down, and waits. And waits. And then he says, "Today, this scripture has been fulfilled in your hearing" (Luke 4:21). Quietly, quietly, Jesus had just overturned the law and started to proclaim a new covenant, a new relationship between God and the world. The tone in the synagogue goes in short order from nice to nasty. The good pious folk in Nazareth think he is being awfully presumptuous, but after all, no prophet is acceptable in his or her own country, and a very unpleasant scene ensues, and Jesus ends up moving to Capernaum. That is not really the point, though. There is something new going on here that had not been done in recent memory. And he goes off preaching and teaching and healing.

Release to captives. Freedom from bondage. Yet, having proclaimed and preached, and taught and healed, there did not (and does not) seem to be much that changed. Wars and rumors of wars still happen. People die in poverty and slavery and people are tortured and unjustly imprisoned. The so-called "Christian right" adds footnotes, laws, and requires blind obedience to the letter of their own law and gives Christianity a bad name. And we trans folk find our own private hell in the bondage of a binary, hetero-patriarchal, sexist gender system. We find our oppression in the intolerance of those who would mark us as sinners, as monsters, as freaks of nature, or worse: as poor, unfortunate, diseased victims of nature or genetics or circumstance.

Paul, in the third chapter of his letter to the Christians in Galatia, says in apparent reference to that new covenant which in his view supplants or fulfills the old, "As many of you as were baptized into Christ have clothed yourselves with Christ. There is no longer Jew or Greek, there is no longer slave or free, there is no longer male and female; for all of you are one in Christ Jesus. And if you belong to Christ, then you are Abraham's offspring, heirs according to the promise" (Gal 3:27–29). It seems the Galatians were concerned, around the year 55 CE, for there were some "Judaizers" who began to teach that it might be necessary to keep the Mosaic law in order to follow the Christian way.

The reference to male and female may be a reference to Gen 1:27: "So God created humankind in his image, in the image of God he created them; male and female he created them." One wonders if Paul was really paying attention when he wrote this letter, and if he was, what precisely he meant to accomplish. For certainly, slavery in many forms, sexuality, sexism, phyletism (ethnocentrism), and chauvinism continue to this very day in all places. Indeed, in his letter to the Christians at Colossae, Paul has specific advice for wives and slaves (Col 3:18–25), so it is hardly likely that he meant to upset the applecart by seriously questioning the system and its tools of oppression. Still, much as one hates to admit it, Paul (in spite of his own sexism) may be on to something here, in this letter to the Galatians, in that a careful distinction must be made between essential actuality and seeming reality.

The discussion at this point in his letter to the Galatians has to do with the idea of freedom, that they have been freed from slavery to a blind and faceless law which stood between them and God. Now that they have the gift of faith, they can stand before God as free, autonomous heirs and children by adoption. The focus is partly on the generosity and love of God in making them (and us) his own. It is this boundless divine love that empowers us, which frees us to be who we truly are, which enables us to begin to see that there is a fundamental actuality that lies behind and above the facade of our present realities.

Within Paul's dialectic on the essential message of the gospel, which has as its primary focus and purpose the freedom and salvation of humanity as aspects or hallmarks of participation in the "kingdom of heaven," it is helpful to note that (from the perspective of Deity, perhaps) it really has no relevance to say that a particular incarnated soul has about it the trappings of sexual identity, involuntary servitude or employment, or ethnicity, for none of these have any impact on the salvation and freedom of the individual soul. Still, it is a hard lesson. In the writings of the Desert Fathers, it is recorded that a traveling monk ran into a party of monastic women. And seeing them, he wanted to avoid temptation and impure thoughts, and so departed from the road. The abbess called out to him, "If you were a perfect monk, you would not even have looked close enough see that we are women."[1] Aside from the abbess calling into the question the matter of sexuality, two matters are implied here: custody of the eyes and *theosis* (becoming godlike). Old monastic custom has it that one exercises custody of the eyes, by which is meant that the monastic does not allow her or his eyes to wander about, but keeps the gaze centered on the path ahead. *Theosis* is involved here in a limited fashion and as an extension of the acquisition of humility and clarity of thought, the idea is that if one is really being about the business of

1. Merton, *Wisdom*, 48.

being a monk, then one is endeavoring to see with the eyes of Divinity; one is trying to see as God sees, and not as a mortal human. Now obviously, few of us are monastics, but the matter is worth considering, for we are all trying to achieve a balanced view of life and a reasonable way to connect earth and heaven.

Over and over again, the gospel writers recount how Jesus had no hesitation in interacting with women, slaves, and pagans. The fourth chapter of St. John's Gospel depicts his interaction with a Samaritan woman, and then, with a Roman official. Two sorts of people any pious Jewish man of that time would scrupulously avoid. Immediately following that he is shown healing an Israelite, but on the Sabbath, in clear violation of the Mosaic law. There he goes again. It was as if these legal matters really did not matter to him, he went right to the heart of the individual and responded with love and compassion to the inmost self, refusing to judge, and giving only the slightest acknowledgement to the social and legal issues having to do with cultural ranking or classification. The realm, which is not of this world, seems to have a different legal system from the Mosaic and pays little attention to the trappings of this world. So too are we called to look beyond the cultural accidents of social presentation, to look beyond the facade of appearance, and to gaze carefully into the eyes and souls of our fellow citizens.

We are called to see others, and ourselves, as God sees us. We are called to that rarefied state described with such beauty and love in the seventeenth chapter of John's Gospel, in which we participate in the life of divinity: seeing, hearing, breathing, praying, and being God. To be one with the Creator through Jesus Christ, God's Son, is to perceive and feel and understand in a new way, in which the essential actuality of persons and situations comes to the foreground, clearly seen and appreciated, while the accidents of social position and class fade into obscurity.

"There is no longer male and female," says Paul (Gal 3:28). As said a moment ago, one wonders what on earth Paul could have been thinking, for it is uncharacteristic of what many of us have come to expect from him, what with his reputation for a

13

misogynistic slant on almost everything. For you see, if there is no longer male and female, then miraculously, no longer is sex and gender an issue. From the perspective of the new covenant, from the perspective of the realm of God, the issues of sexuality, sexual orientation, and gender identity are not fit subjects to impede our relationship with God, with each other, or with ourselves, with our very selves. These are just some of the matters governed by the Mosaic law, and for all of his attitude, Paul caught on to the idea that blind obedience to law was incompatible with service in the new realm of God proclaimed and established by Jesus. For God, indeed, is truly a God of love and not of severity and judgement.

It is said that in the desert, Abbot Lot once came to Abbot Joseph to ask what he might do to live his life as well as he is able. He had a rule of life which involved prayer, fasting, meditation, and silence. As Thomas Merton relates the incident, the elder rose up in reply and stretched out his hands to heaven, and his fingers became like ten lamps of fire. He said, "Why not be totally changed into fire?"[2] Why indeed, for fire is in our very souls, it is at the root of the very essence of our beings, it is the spark of divinity resident in our hearts.

That fire might be associated with divinity is not new, although popular mythology tends, at least since Dante, to connect fire with purgation and judgement. Still, as early as the book of Deuteronomy, it is written that "the Lord your God is a devouring fire" (Deut 4:24). Abbess Hildegard of Bingen, in the twelfth century, said that God is "the supreme fire; not deadly, but rather, enkindling every spark of life." It is that radiant fire of divinity that supports and sustains all of creation. There is, she says, "No creation that does not have [this] radiance, be it greenness or seed, blossom or beauty." The Holy Spirit of God, she continues, "is a Burning Spirit. It kindles the hearts of humankind. Like tympanum and lyre it plays them, gathering volume in the temple of the soul. . . . Radiant life, worthy of all praise, the Holy Spirit resurrects and awakens everything that is. Truly, the Holy Spirit is an

2. Merton, *Wisdom*, 58.

unquenchable fire."[3] The ground of our being, therefore, is divinity. The Holy Spirit is specifically that divinity which is the eternal and abiding presence of God in creation. It is worth reflection to note that in Greek it is a feminine noun, and in Hebrew the word for that Divine presence is *Shekhinah*, another feminine noun.

In his edition of the *Zohar*, Scholem spends some time with the idea of the scholar's relationship to both the Torah as well as the *Shekhinah*, pointing to the notion that the relationship is indeed that of the lover for the beloved.[4] In his earlier work, *Major Trends in Jewish Mysticism*, he discusses at some considerable length the kabalistic view of the symbolic relationship between sexuality, sensuality, and Divinity, noting that in Divinity was to be discerned the union of these forces.[5] Indeed, he noted that there is a dynamic relationship between Divinity and humanity, between creator and created, which has sexuality as its analogue. And in fact, Origen, Bernard of Clairvaux, and the Targum are in substantial agreement in their interpretations of the Song of Songs of King Solomon, that this work is a symbolic representation of the history of God's relationship with Israel, or for Christian apologists, with the church. Again, there is the assumption that there is some aspect of the relationship that may be understood in terms of sexuality but combined with an unfortunate bias toward and assumption of heterosexuality, which can profitably be ignored.

It is important that we do not get too literal with this stuff. Remember we are talking not in terms of hard and fast definitions, not in terms of essential or substantial categories, but rather in terms of metaphor, of analogue, and of symbolic representations. Remember that symbolism, poetry, and music are part of the soul's language, not rhetoric or geometry, and we are talking in terms of soul, spirituality, and ultimate realities. For trans folk in particular, but certainly for anyone, it may be useful as well to remember that in Divinity there is the dynamic union of these aspects, and moreover, that we humans are made in the image and likeness of

---

3. Hildegard, "Meditation: Hildegard of Bingen."

4. Scholem, *Zohar*, 112.

5. Scholem, *Mysticism*, 325.

that Divinity, and so we are called to reflect the union of these aspects in our own lives. Indeed, we are called to what amounts to a higher consciousness, a clearer vision in which sexual orientation, sexuality, and gender identification are no longer relevant, by virtue of our adoption as free children of God with citizenship in the new realm.

Very early on, perhaps in the first or second century of the Common Era, the anonymous author of the letter to Diognetus wrote, in an explanation of the Christian way, that Christians live in the world as if they were just passing through, as if they were peaceful resident aliens, citizens of another place.[6] Now, this is not to presume to suggest a pie in the sky kind of eschatology, where we talk about how someday our ship will come in, or someday the revolution will happen, or someday Jesus will come again, and then all these awful, worldly encumbrances and heartaches will disappear. No, not at all. Perhaps it is more along the lines that we recognize the evanescent and nebulous nature of the present and realize that the gospel message calls us to a higher consciousness, to an apprehension and appreciation of our freedom to connect to an essential actuality, the like of which is only occasionally hinted at by those who write of the higher mysteries, and now and then written about or commented upon by philosophers and preachers.

Issues having to do with the world have their place, certainly, and no doubt have some impact on our ability to go from one day to the next. Even if we should come to believe in our hearts that this world is nothing but a sea of illusion (which may not be entirely accurate either), we still find it necessary to make a living in it and to interact with other people in it. So in fact these very matters need not and cannot be stumbling blocks to our development of loving and lasting relationships. In coming to a better understanding of them, according to the terms of the realm of God, we are empowered to be creative and to develop new ways of coping and interacting with the world. Thus it is that the author of the letter to Diognetus said that Christians, indistinguishable from others either by nationality, language, or customs, play their full role as

6. "Epistle of Mathetes," ch. 5.

citizens but labor under all the disabilities of aliens, obedient to the laws, they yet live on a level that transcends the law.[7]

So therefore, far from being an issue which divides us and separates us from the love of God, this matter of living as a trans person can be settled. The matter will never be entirely closed, for each one, each generation will wrestle and argue, contend, and theorize about these issues anew. Still, we may take comfort in hearing Jesus as he echoed the words of the prophet Isaiah, saying, "the Spirit of the Lord is upon me, because he has anointed me to bring good news to the poor. He has sent me to proclaim release to the captives and recovery of sight to the blind, to let the oppressed go free, to proclaim the acceptable year of the Lord's favor" (Luke 4:18–19). It is not a matter to impede our relations with God or with each other.

There is neither male nor female, for we are all one in Christ Jesus, released from the bondage and oppression of an obsolete system of arbitrarily imposed, restrictive categories, released from the notion that blind obedience to law could ever be better than clear-sighted understanding and personal responsibility. If we are Christ's, then we are Abraham's offspring, heirs according to promise. Let us pray for the vision, the insight to see that in the kingdom whose *dynamis* (or energy, or spirit) is that which is fully realized here among us, and yet at the same time not yet accomplished, there is in fact no longer Jew or Greek, there is no longer slave or free, there is no longer male and female. Let us pray for the strength to bring that realization so deeply into our lives that we can live at peace with ourselves and with others and with the God who has released us from bondage, who has given us the freedom of the inheritance of that kingdom.

7. "Epistle of Mathetes," ch. 5.

3

Death, Burial, and Life

Homily given on March 13, 2005, at Dignity New York City[1]
(Ezekiel 37:1–14; Romans 15:1–13; John 11:1–44)

THIS IS SUCH A great story. The temptation, with the story of the death and raising of Lazarus, is naturally to make reference to Jesus telling one of three unmarried siblings to come out.

I wonder what it was like for Lazarus. He had gone through all the trouble of dying, and was quietly dead, and then suddenly his old friend Jesus called him back to life. Although certainly being alive is really good, we like to tell ourselves that when we die it will be better, because we will be with God in that place where there is no pain, or suffering, or death. Unless of course we are in purgatory . . . but even that is not so bad, at least according to Aquinas, because we are beyond time and we know with enormous certainty that once we finish there, we will be in heaven with God. Now, for Lazarus, wherever he was, he was pulled back to

---

1. Dignity is the national US organization for LGBTQ Roman Catholics. Find them at www.dignity.com.

earthly life, and as good as that is, he would have to go through dying all over again.

The stories in the gospel provide an interesting progression. In the first, you recall, there was a little girl who had just died, and Jesus said she had just fallen asleep. "Little girl, arise," he said, and took her by the hand, and she got up (Mark 5:41). And, like a good Jewish uncle, he told them to give her something to eat. Then, elsewhere, entering the town of Nain, he saw the people bringing out the body of a man to bury it, the only son of a widowed mother, and he saw the man's mother. Jesus, the son of a widowed mother himself, perhaps with an understanding of how his own career would end, brought the man back from death and gave him to his mother (Luke 7:11–17). He had probably been dead for at least a few hours. Now, we have Lazarus, who has been dead for three or four days, and has already been entombed. (The tradition is that the soul lurks around the body for three days after death . . . so clearly, Lazarus is really dead.) Now on the one hand, it must clearly be seen as an affirmation of our historic faith in the resurrection of the body, but on the other hand, we must hear another call to identify our individual deaths and burials. As people of trans experience, we sometimes talk of the "dead name," and we may have made significant efforts to bury that prior name and identity, in order to live more fully and authentically in the present.

It is so easy to take the discussions of death as if they are allegories. The first reading, from the sixth century BC prophet Ezekiel, is addressed to the captives in Babylon, and it is generally seen as an allegory for the return of Israel from captivity, with their political existence and hope entirely restored. Following on the very well-known passage about the valley of dry bones, God will give us life and have us rise from our graves, will bring us back from exile and give us a good, green land in which to live in peace. For Ezekiel, it was a lost cause; the whole house of Israel was living in exile, and there was evidently no hope for the future. Imagine how it must be, alienated from dreams and hopes for the future. For us too, here in this place, we may find ourselves wondering about our hopes and dreams, concerned that our own choices and options have been limited by others, acting out of fear, prejudice, even hatred. Dignity and the many other organizations that promote justice and renewal within the church have all been around for an awfully long time, and it must seem at times like the dream of reconciliation and justice has been deferred indefinitely for LG-BTQ people, women, and religiously progressive people.

There are times when each of us must feel that we are buried in our studies, in our jobs, in our families, so buried, that we feel that we cannot get out. That theme of exile, from Ezekiel, is one that recurs in our Christian tradition. Early on, as you probably know, a number of faithful left the cities and went into voluntary exile, to the deserts of Egypt, or to Persia and Assyria (present day Iran and Iraq), to die there, to die to the world, to self will, and to sin. They also considered themselves dead to their families, friends, and communities, in order to live for Christ and in Christ.

There are two aspects of this theme of death and burial. In the first, we are exiled from God, buried in the passing cares of this world, buried by oppression, alienation, and rejection. So many of us feel this in our work or personal situations, knowing that we have to find a way out. There can be no doubt that Jesus had enormous sympathy for those of us who feel trapped in situations that we cannot control, and through the words of the prophet he reassures us that he will deliver us from our captivity and bring us into a good, green land—into a good life with him. He is the way out. For those of us who feel like we are struggling uphill, he is the way out.

Another aspect is that of voluntary exile for the sake of the realm of God, for the sake of some great goal, some great ideal, some genuine purpose. In last week's Gospel, the disciples asked about the man born blind, and Jesus said that it was to enable the manifestation of God's glory. Here too, we have a sense of purpose in Lazarus's dying. Over the centuries, martyrs die for something, and there is a sense that there are consequences for their deaths. In our own time, the deaths of Martin Luther King Jr., John F. Kennedy, Bobby Kennedy, and Malcolm X all had consequences. On a more local level, each of our deaths brings us closer to justice.

The pain of the deaths from AIDS, the impact of hepatitis C, and crystal meth on our community, and the consecration of Episcopal Bishop Gene Robinson in New Hampshire, all point to a greater issue, the promise of a resurrection that is greater, a liberation from oppression.

Here in New York, there are those of us who voluntarily give of ourselves for the realization of some great goal. There were those who took part in June 1969, in the Stonewall Rebellion, and in the early gay rights movement. Risking alienation from family and community, some of us are committed to the ministries of prophetic witness and irritation of those in authority, in support of the movement for marriage equality, and to the various campaigns for equal treatment under the law, for domestic partnership benefits, for the ordination of women and married people in the Roman church, or even for the full inclusion of LGBTQ people in the city's parade on Saint Patrick's Day. Sometimes, the ministry of irritation is helpful, and sometimes it is the ministry of quiet persistence and prayer. Here, in Ezekiel's words, we have the assurance that our exile will end, and that we will be brought back with joy to the community of the living. Whatever it is that separates us from happiness, whatever it is that buries us in worries and cares, we have the assurance that Jesus understands that situation.

The sense of exile and alienation, of burial, can also be something about us. The letter to the Romans makes the interesting point that a lot of our alienation is due to our long standing tendency to live out of harmony with God's will. But by virtue of our baptism and the indwelling of the Holy Spirit, even though we experience sickness and death, we have the assurance of eternal life. Paul advances the discourse, moving it from dying and rising to new life in Christ, focusing on resurrection and a future hope, to the more immediate concern of living today in Christ's life, with the Holy Spirit dwelling in each of us. By so doing, he backs up into a consideration of Christian life in the here and now, in community, in the community of believers. For Paul, it may be that we are already living in the resurrection, in the kingdom of God. It may be that the household of faith is the realized household of

God. The idea of resurrection is not only a future promise, but a present reality. We are living the resurrection now—restored, forgiven, reconciled.

For Christians who observe the Julian calendar (most Orthodox, the Armenians, the Oriental Orthodox, and the Assyrian Church of the East), this year of 2005, Lent actually begins this evening. Forgiveness Vespers is celebrated in Orthodox parishes, and during the course of the service, everyone in the parish asks everyone else, one-on-one, one by one, for forgiveness for any faults, and it is in this process of forgiveness that we have another way out. The perception and experience of alienation and exile are common to us all, and yet through the sacraments—particularly the sacraments of the Eucharist and Reconciliation—through the work of the Holy Spirit in the sacraments, we have the assurance of forgiveness, pardon, and restoration, and that in the end all will be well. Lent is a great time for introspection, it is a time for us to look at the tombs in which we find ourselves buried.

My brothers and sisters, we have here in this place the offer and opportunity to emerge from our burial and exile. In the sacraments, in the calendar, in the coming celebration of the Feast of Feasts, of Easter, in the community of believers, we are called out of our tombs into the light of day.

4

Duality: A Divided Life

WHEN I WAS LITTLE, I remember my father telling me that his grandmother, when she was a little girl, met Abraham Lincoln, who gave her a penny. This was really a very big deal for me, particularly because we were in the middle of taking notice of the centenary of the American Civil War, and I was in the middle of being totally infatuated with television portrayals of Mr. Lincoln. In one of those portrayals, I recall him quoting Jesus saying, "Every kingdom divided against itself is laid waste, and no city or house divided against itself will stand" (Matt 12:25). Now it seems to me that this is a useful bit of grist for the mill of thought about living from day-to-day as a trans person.

Among ourselves we often refer to "living full-time," as if that were innately superior to "living part-time." Both of these are shorthand forms, of course, and they refer to living full or part-time in the gender role most suited to the individual. For most of us, this gender role is ordinarily not the one society would incline to associate with one's genital landscape, and hence our various dilemmas. Anyway, what strikes me most forcibly in these expressions is the notion that it is possible for one to *live* full-time or part-time. If one lives only part-time, then what of the rest of the time?

A friend of mine lives part-time; at work and at a class in grad school she presents mostly as masculine, while the rest of her life she lives as herself. A house divided against itself cannot stand. In her divided life she feels acutely the pressure to conform her behavior to gender-based stereotypes which numb the mind and deaden the soul. Faced with the certainty of losing her employment and the consequent economic devastation for her family, she often dances with depression and entertains the prospect of hastening her own death. A house divided against itself cannot stand. For her, the pain of living only part-time is very nearly unbearable, while the consequences of honesty and congruity are catastrophic. She lives only part-time, and she dies part-time. While she lives, she has the prospect of death constantly before her eyes. And while her life leaks away, eight hours a day, nine-to-five, she has the vision and the promise of living authentically ever in mind.

This pain is not unique to trans folk, by any means. Another friend of mine is in a committed relationship with another woman, and together they have two fine sons. On her desk are photos of her boys but not of her partner, for she too is faced with the certainty of job loss and economic devastation for her family if she dares to disclose her departure from those heterosexist stereotypes. She lives part-time, a divided life, and she dies an inch at a time every moment of every work day, waiting for that day when justice, peace, and mercy truly reign, when each of us enjoys equality and has the freedom to live and love, to work and worship according to God's plan for us, according to God's love for us in our infinite diversity and complexity.

Offsetting this focus on internal division is Jesus's observation about loyalties, associations, and alliances. Luke's Gospel shows him saying, "No slave can serve two masters: for a slave will either hate the one and love the other, or be devoted to the one and despise the other" (Luke 16:13). Specifically applicable to the situation in which we find ourselves as trans people, it is just this problem with splitting, dividing, or balancing our loyalties or even our identities, as it were, that propels many of us to transition: it is natural for us to prefer one master to another, and it is natural for us to be troubled by the task of serving two masters. While it is not an impossible task for some trans people, it is intolerably difficult for others for whom it feels like a betrayal of their true identities.

This change in life and lifestyle is not without precedent in Scripture or in history, and it is most often accompanied by a change of name as well as a sense of having been called apart for a particular mission or ministry. The patriarch Abraham was once known as Abram; Israel was known as Jacob; and it is not recorded whether Moses had a different name before he was named by the daughter of the Pharaoh at the age of three months. A change of name, whether the change is announced by God or by another, is an outward sign of a change in status, a change in one's life goals, in one's identity.

In Christian times, Simon became Peter, Saul became Paul, and in the Christian monastic tradition one enters religious life with a new name. All of these witness to the sense of the individual's having been reborn, or born again, called to a new life of simplicity, of unity, of love, and of service. For some transgender women and men, the life shift is not less than a complete rebirth to a hope of life now integrated, undivided, and peaceful, now with new challenges, new visions, and new attitudes. This is of course certainly not ever to imply that post-transition life is inevitably always better; homophobia and transphobia still lead to hate crimes and too many people are woefully ignorant of our situations and so in their fear and distress find it necessary to attack and vilify us.

For some of us, in the trangender life-experience, the question of spirituality often arises in connection with the journey itself and with the changing relationship of the individual with her or his body, family, and social circle. As with Abraham, there is the sense for many of us of having been called to journey far from one's place of origin to begin a new life and to initiate a new personal history qualitatively different from the former life. Francis of Assisi, Mary of Egypt, and Augustine of Hippo all knew this call, this rebirth to a new life, and inevitably it signaled the reorientation of their lives in the direction of personal fulfillment, self-actualization, and the pursuit of wisdom.

No doubt there must have been a concomitant sense of nostalgia for former lives, for all new beginnings have their difficulties, and the good old days always seem at times to have been easier, friendlier, or better. No doubt there must have been fear of the consequences of the choice to enter a new life, and no doubt the fears and misgivings must have been reasonable and accurate. Still, for each of them, there was an act of faith growing out of a gift of faith. For many of us too, the key to our survival is faith, for "faith is the assurance of things hoped for, the conviction of things not seen" (Heb 11:1).

One of the good things about reading the lives of the saints is the realization that they lived lives like ours and they finally succeeded. One of the good things about sharing our personal stories with each other is that we realize that for most of us, our stories are the same. It gets better, and there comes a sense of integration, of unity, and of restoration; a sense that our faith was not idle nor was it in vain.

5

Forgiveness, Generosity, and Love

Homily given on February 11, 2007, at Dignity New York City
(Jeremiah 17:5–11; 1 Corinthians 15:12–19; Luke 6:17–26)

I HAVE TO SAY I have been wrestling with these scriptures all week,
because I have been hoping somehow to connect them somehow
with the start of national marriage equality week and Valentine's
Day. We shall see. You may have to trust me to get us there. In
these weeks following the celebration of Epiphany, we have looked
at the many ways that Jesus revealed himself, his mission, and his
message to the world.

Now, we see him in the middle of his earthly ministry, with a
whole multitude of people who were listening to him. One immediate reaction, of course, is that he cannot possibly be talking to us,
now, in the twenty-first century, living in one of the richest cities,
in one of the richest nations, on the planet. Another immediate reaction might be, if he *is* talking to us, we are in some deep trouble.
It must have been similar for some of those who were present that
day. Certainly, not everyone in the crowd was poor; there must
have been some wealthy people there, for it is written that they had

come from all over Judea and Jerusalem, from the seacoast of Tyre and Sidon, to hear him and be healed of their diseases.

Why did they stay and listen? In two verses just before the part we read this evening, it is said that they came to be healed of their diseases and released from torment by unclean spirits, and they were healed. It says they all sought to touch him, for power went out from him and healed them all. Not only did he heal them, but he also took the opportunity to talk with them, to comfort them, to challenge them. Peculiarly, his approach was not simply to comfort the afflicted and afflict the comfortable. At first glance, it seems that he is afflicting everyone. Practically, to say to someone "blessed are you who hunger now, for you will be filled" (Luke 6:21) . . . later . . . is rather like the Epistle of St. James, when he warns the readers that it is really not good enough to say to those who are naked and destitute of daily food, "Go in peace! Be warm and eat your fill" (James 2:16) without actually lifting a hand to do something to help by giving them what they need.

The promise of a reward after we die cannot possibly be what Jesus is offering here. Nor can it be that he is really telling those who have wealth or happiness that it will not last, even if, as we know, it is really true. No, though he certainly may be warning us not to depend on wealth or to presume that popularity is necessarily a mark of holiness.

Right after this, Jesus gets more specific: "But I say to you that listen: Love your enemies, do good to those who hate you, bless those who curse you, pray for those who abuse you. If anyone strikes you on the cheek, offer the other also; and from anyone who takes away your cloak, do not withhold even your shirt. Give to everyone who begs from you" (Luke 6:27–30a).

These Beatitudes, these sayings of Jesus, are so familiar. For some, they are a description of what the Christian life is, or should be, while for others they are a series of peculiar paradoxes—especially this version in Luke's Gospel, with its four blessings and four woes, or four warnings, and its talk of forgiveness, generosity, and love for our enemies. It seems oddly appropriate to link this reading with that from the prophet Jeremiah, with his similar pairing:

"Cursed are those who trust in mere mortals and make mere flesh their strength, whose hearts turn away from the Lord. . . . Blessed are those who trust in the Lord, whose trust is the Lord" (Jer 17:5, 7). Appropriate too to link it with the first psalm of David, with the same kind of themes and contrasts.

In the Eastern church, this is Meatfare Sunday, leading up to the entry into Lent, and it is oddly coincidental that the reading for the day is from Matthew's Gospel, chapter 25, the separation of the sheep and the goats at the last day. There we find the famous lines to those on his right hand: "Come, you that are blessed by my Father, inherit the kingdom prepared for you from the foundation of the world; for I was hungry and you gave me food; I was thirsty and you gave me something to drink; I was a stranger and you welcomed me; I was naked and you gave me clothing; I was sick and you took care of me; I was in prison and you visited me" (Matt 25:34–36). Clearly, in this recollection of the blessing of those who are generous and the condemnation of those who have no regard for others, the church—East and West—would have us consider the immediate and long term implications of our relationships, as individuals, as communities, and as nations.

Nearly one hundred years ago, in his *Seven Pillars of Wisdom*, T. E. Lawrence, usually known as Lawrence of Arabia,[1] made an interesting observation about Semitic discourse: he said that Semites were bred in the desert to see things in black and white and to ignore the grays. He said they would prefer seemingly contradictory statements forming a paradoxical expression of truth to a carefully nuanced and qualified precision within a single statement of fact. Better to acknowledge the fundamental mystery than to attempt to define what cannot be defined.

The great mystery that we really cannot quite wrap our heads around is that the Bible is a love story, that what we used to call "salvation history" is a love story, and that God loved us all into being and continues to love us in every moment of every day of our lives. The prophet Jeremiah and the psalmist acknowledge that from the earliest times, there were problems: jealousy, infidelity,

1. Lawrence, *Wisdom*, 38.

greed; and in response God sent the prophets, again and again . . . and again and again God's people put their trust in political alliances and foreign gods.

God calls to us through one voice or another. "Cursed is the one who trusts in men, whose heart turns away from God" (Jer 17:5), and again, "blessed is the one who trusts in God, whose hope is in the Almighty." (Jer 17:7) Paul, in his letter to the Corinthians, echoes this when he says, "If for this life only we have hoped in Christ, we are the most pitiable people of all" (1 Cor 15:19). Christianity is more than an ethical system, it is participation in Christ's life, death, resurrection, and eternal life. In our lives here and now, we encounter one another and we are called to enter into relationship with one another, acknowledging that fundamentally, we are not separate but united together in Christ. If Christianity is anything it is love: love in action, love in relationship, love going out to serve, love sacrificing itself, love rooted in the love of Christ, who came not to be served but to serve, and to give his life as a ransom for many.

There are always the great and large ways of serving. Father Damien of Molokai, who served the lepers and who contracted the disease himself, is one. Mother Theresa of Calcutta is another. But service is not just for heroes and saints. Each of us is called to serve others, in our relationships, families, jobs, that Christ may finally greet us and say, "Come, you that are blessed by my Father, inherit the kingdom prepared for you from the foundation of the world; for I was hungry and you gave me food; I was thirsty and you gave me something to drink; I was a stranger and you welcomed me; I was naked and you gave me clothing; I was sick and you took care of me; I was in prison and you came to me" (Matt 25:34–36).

John's Gospel records no Eucharist, but he describes the foot-washing that we reenact every year on Holy Thursday. Jesus said to them, "Do you know what I have done to you? You call me Teacher and Lord; and you are right, for that is what I am. So if I, your Lord and Teacher, have washed your feet, you also ought to wash one another's feet. For I have set you an example that you should do as I have done to you"(John 13:13–14).

We are called to serve one another, to clean up after one another, to look out for one another, to speak up for one another, and to help one another. Particularly as LGBTQ people, we experience marginalization, alienation, and separation, and we are called to build a web of relationships, a community grounded in loving service, "For I have given you an example, that you should do as I have done to you" (John 13:14). What does it take, what does it mean, to look after one another when the other is the oppressor, is homophobic, transphobic, or a terrorist? What if the other is someone whose values are not ours?

It is not that God does not want us to be happy or satisfied, but that God wants all of us to be happy and satisfied, and until that happens, our hearts will be restless, for the human heart is to mirror the heart of God with a love that goes out to others.

In our lives, in our families, and in our communities, we are called, as the Prophet Micah says, to do justice, love mercy (or in some translations to love well), and walk humbly with God (Mic 6:8). In this call, we find our way not only to Valentine's Day, but to a recognition that marriage equality, and equality in general, but especially here in this community, for LGBTQ people, is without question what God has in mind for each of us.

In the end, we are called to perfection, to perfect life, love, and kindness. We are called to commit ourselves, and one another, and all our life, to Christ our God. If we turn our life over to God, allowing God to change us, transform us, live in us, and perfect us, we act as God's children, as faithful followers of Jesus, and we become walking valentines, deeply in love with God, and with one another.

6

Community, Relationships, and Commitment (Ruth 1)

REMEMBER IN *FIDDLER ON the Roof* when Tevye asks his good wife of many years if she loves him? She tells him all she has done for him and for their family, and he asks again, and so it goes. And finally she says yes, she loves him. Do you recall how finally it was not about doing, about activity at all, but rather it was about being? See, they had had no opportunity to commit to each other. The marriage had been arranged, and in all probability they first met on their wedding day. They were expected to give it all they had, to give the relationship all it took to succeed. So they had kids, got to know each other, set up housekeeping, kept the Sabbath, and did all the good things they were expected to do. But it was not about doing things. The potter is not the clay and we are not our deeds. Did they love each other? This is not a foolish question, but a very real one. What if she said no? What if he looked within himself, within his own soul, and said no? A bill of divorce was always a possibility, or they could just decide to live together in moderately comfortable, peaceful coexistence. By now they probably were comfortable together, if not altogether happy, and certainly after a fashion they loved their children and their home/life/lifestyle. But in this instance, they did indeed love each other, love and intimacy had grown between them, not merely a feeling but rather a deep sense of unity, maintained by the will and strengthened by habit, and reinforced with the support of their families and community, and the loving hand of God.

Love in an intentional community, in a family, involves loving in the context of the mundane, the ordinary, the unremarkable. Yet it is just this loving that is so tremendously sanctifying. Toward the end of his Gospel, John recounts that before the feast of the Passover, during supper, Jesus stood up and laid aside his garments, and girded himself with a towel. Then he poured water into a basin, and began to wash the disciples' feet, and to wipe them with the towel (John 13:1–5). Love and commitment are found and nourished most often in the ordinary, in the routines which frame our daily lives. It is found in the selfless service we give each other. Dirty laundry, budget problems, taxes, illness, and conflicts, the tears and laughter of each day contribute the setting for our growth together. Love has no price tag, and in relation to others love implies a striving for oneness of mind, heart, and spirit, letting go of self-centeredness. It involves the free and unconditional gift of oneself, rather than a contract with rights and duties.

In an earlier time, long ago, in the days when the judges ruled, there was a famine in the land, and a certain man of Bethlehem in Judah went to sojourn in the country of Moab—he and his wife, Naomi, and their two sons. And he died, and his two sons, who had both married, died also. So Naomi decided to return to her family in Bethlehem and she told her daughters-in-law to return to their families among the Moabite people. One of them, whose name was Ruth, said, "Do not press me to leave you or turn back from following you! Where you go I will go; where you lodge I will lodge; your people shall be my people, and your God my God. Where you die I will die—there will I be buried. May the Lord do thus and so to me, and more as well, if even death parts me from you!" (Ruth 1:16–17). The short chronicle of Ruth and Naomi is a tale of love and faithfulness.

"Ah, you are beautiful, my love; ah, you are beautiful; your eyes are doves. . . . You have ravished my heart, my sister, my bride, you have ravished my heart with a glance of your eyes. . . . How sweet is your love, my sister, my bride! How much better is your love than wine, and the fragrance of your oils than any spice" (Song 1:15; 4:9a, 10). Love and faithfulness have little to do with logic. In matters of the heart, in matters of the spirit, rationality and pragmatism are rarely applicable. By the same token, as C. S. Lewis pointed out in *Mere Christianity*, there is the false and irrational notion that love and faithfulness, once discovered, will never change.[1] Living happily ever after does not necessarily mean feeling the same way, experiencing the same thrills in the same way, day after day.

In the days of Samuel the prophet, Samuel was sent to Jesse to anoint one of his sons to be king over Israel, and God revealed to him that it was to be David. It is recorded that David "was ruddy, and had beautiful eyes, and was handsome" (1 Sam 16:12). David was anointed by Samuel and some time later David entered Saul's household staff. Still later, David returned from the slaughter of Goliath the Philistine and spoke to King Saul. When he had finished speaking it is recorded that the soul of Jonathan (Saul's son and heir) "was bound to the soul of David, and Jonathan loved him as his own soul. Saul took him that day and would not let him return to his father's house. Then Jonathan made a covenant with David because he loved him as his own soul" (1 Sam 18:1–3). Here too is the story of the birth and growth of love, devotion, and faithfulness.

"Upon my bed at night I sought him whom my soul loves. . . . My beloved is all radiant and ruddy, distinguished among ten thousand. His head is the finest gold; his locks are wavy, black as a raven. . . . This is my beloved and this is my friend" (Song 3:1; 5:10–11, 16b). We love our friends, we love our partners and spouses, not for what they have done, but for who they are. Not for their background, ethnicity, or expression of gender, but for the immortal spark of divinity as it is expressed in their souls. We love them, not for their capabilities, their brilliance, their dependability, or even for their courage. Not for being butch or femme. These

1. Lewis, *Christianity*, 99.

attributes, sterling though they may be, do not and cannot constitute a justification for love and cannot sustain a relationship. For love is not a matter of the head but the heart. A good friend and former associate, walking with me once in the East Village (of New York City), remarked that to find love in this broken world was certainly one of the greatest of miracles, and together we paused in silent thanks for this gift of God.

John, the disciple whom Jesus loved, recounts that after the resurrection, one morning after breakfast by the Sea of Tiberias, Jesus said a peculiar thing to Peter: "Simon son of John, do you love me?" Peter replied, "Yes, Lord; you know that I love you," and Jesus said, "Feed my lambs" (John 21:15). Love talk. Now remember, this was the same Peter who had run away, the same Peter who had denied Jesus, the same Peter who had lost his temper and cut off a servant's ear, the same Peter who it may be presumed had left his family and mother-in-law to wander around Galilee with Jesus. The same Peter who heard Jesus say to the disciples, not many days before, "As the Creator has loved me, so have I loved you; abide in my love. . . . This is my commandment, love one another as I have loved you. . . . You did not choose me, but I chose you and appointed you that you should go and bear fruit and that your fruit should abide" (John 15:9, 12, 16). Perhaps particularly for John, love is both the seed and the fruit of our life together, of our lives as children of God. Relationships are not built on deeds or reputation, but on the innate individuality and personhood of the builders.

In his book, *The Different Drum*, M. Scott Peck notes that "trapped in our tradition of rugged individualism, we are an extraordinarily lonely people. So lonely, in fact, that many cannot even acknowledge their loneliness to themselves, much less to others."[2] We yearn for connection, for mutuality, for community, but we find all too often that we are trapped within a kind of prison of our own making. In our fast-paced society, we have no time for others. The relationships we form are often shallow and tend to superficiality, owing to our wish to form friendships quickly and

2. Peck, *Different Drum*, 58.

easily without much personal investment of time, resources, or self. Western society has taken a turn towards the intensely private. The news media stirs up our fears of the stranger and we lock our physical and emotional doors and forget that Jesus identified with the outsider, the sick, the prisoner, the stranger. "I was a stranger and you welcomed me" (Matt 25:35). We are still called, as were the disciples in John's Gospel, like Jesus, to be foot washers, to take care of each other in a direct and personal way. We are called, like Jesus, to extend hospitality, to work to build community, and to build relationships.

In *Care of the Soul*, Thomas More notes that the "soul longs for attachment, for variety in personality, for intimacy and particularity," and these are the qualities that we seek in community and in each other.[3] Too often we find that what we seek in our relationships, however, is conformity. In seeking conformity in relationship and in ourselves, we are tempted to suppress our own individualities. We hesitate to share our own stories for we fear not fitting in, we fear rejection, and we fear that very variety and particularity for which we yearn. Small talk is the enemy of community and of relationship. So often we seek to form connections in precisely the wrong way, for we expect to make connections with the very souls of other people by talking about politics, activism, current events, sports, and about anything but ourselves. The key to personality, indeed, the key to understanding the world today, does not lie in the "secondary source" recounting of history. It lies rather in "primary sources"—biography and autobiography. It lies in the emotional and personal aspects, the varied hues of the tapestries of our lives. Our connection with the heart of the living God lies not in abstract theology but in personal, spontaneous prayer to that living God, in the face of God seen in other people, and in the Holy Scripture which nourishes us with the personal stories of salvation history. Our connection with each other lies not in their intellectual portrait but in contact and conversation with them, as well as in the stories of their lives, the intimate details of their personal struggles, the questions, and the heartaches.

3. Moore, *Care*, 92.

A professor of my acquaintance pointed out that American literature is most notable in that it has not yet produced a really significant fictional work about relationships. Moreover, good dialogue is not a hallmark of American literature; we are not very good at articulating or portraying relationships. We have tremendous difficulty in describing the dynamic intimate interplay of personality, of friendship, and of desire. By and large, the characters we admire most in literature are solitary characters, loners, and isolated people of few if any words. Heroes and antiheroes are people who are known, indeed who are renowned not for who they are, but for their accomplishments. It is interesting and disappointing that our progressive western culture is so caught up in acts, in individualism, and in social utility that we seem to have little time for a consideration of such a very fundamental cultural phenomenon as the care and maintenance, the pain and joy of relationship. It is likewise disappointing that our culture places so little value on age, wisdom, selflessness, and faithfulness. Most often the value of a person, in society at large, in business, or even in the most intimate of personal relationships, is a function of that person's utility. This reduction of the person to the level of a commodity demeans our common humanity while at the same time it blinds us to each other's fundamental humanity, and we view ourselves and each other as nothing more than slaves, without souls, even without individuality.

For Ruth and Naomi, for David and Jonathan, and for any of us who are blessed with the fullness of an intimate and loving relationship, the real, essential key is not what you have done, but who are you. Relationship is irrational, it flies in the face of our materialistic, pragmatic, utilitarian culture. A good relationship brings us back to some very basic issues having to do with our simplicity and honesty and relies on our willingness (or ability!) to communicate, to really work at building and sustaining a relationship. For again, even the communication of personal philosophies and ideas can actually obstruct the building of relationship in that it can divert the focus away from the person and toward the definition, measurement, and evaluation of the component parts of the person, as if to presume that the person or the relationship, once defined, would be locked in and no longer subject to any change or evolution. Many of us retreat into intellect this way, in order to avoid engaging on an emotional or spiritual level. Others, just as interested in avoidance, escape into sensuality and sexuality, with the same resulting aridity of spirit, the same emotional isolation, and the same loneliness and alienation.

Intimacy is far from easily attained. A community, family, couple, or individual striving for closeness and warmth easily hides disagreements rather than bringing them out in the open where they can be worked through. M. Scott Peck describes the stages of growth of a group and in *The Different Drum* refers to the stage of pseudo-community in this context.[4] To assure peace, we seek people like ourselves, we fail to welcome the stranger, and we fail to allow the stranger in each of us to emerge. With the best of intentions, we violate each other regularly, we reject differences, and we engage in power games. Yet, conflict and contradiction are integral and essential aspects of relationships, and in them we are challenged to abandon illusions about ourselves and others. If the commitment to remain together is sufficiently strong, because of a strong ideology or loyalty, the relationship can grow and evolve, despite (or through) the diversity, conflict, chaos, and emptiness.

None of this happens overnight. Relationship takes time and patience. It is said that Hildegard of Bingen, the noted twelfth century mystic, visionary, author, musician, and scientist, studied with the Abbess Jutta for more than twenty-four years, and in that time they grew to be "soul-friends." In our modern Western culture, twenty-four minutes is a long time. We expect a microwave oven's ability to deliver a piping hot friendship, along with the dinner, in ten minutes. Her biographer, Godfrey, records that Jutta was her mentor and her teacher, as well as her spiritual mother and confidante. In *Praying with Hildegard of Bingen*, Gloria Durka writes that mentors and friends serve as mirrors to help us see ourselves as God sees us: as beloved, unique, and valuable people.[5] As men-

4. Peck, *Different Drum*, 86.
5. Durka, *Hildegard*, 39.

tors they provide counsel, support, and challenge, while as friends they exchange affection, acceptance, and consolation. When Jutta died, Hildegard was unanimously elected by the community at Bingen to succeed her as Abbess. Their friendship was a blessed gift and Hildegard willingly acknowledged the profound influence of Jutta upon her life. We trans folk have a good understanding of mentorship, for it is part and parcel of nearly every social and support group's agenda, it is fundamental to the trans community that we are here to mentor each other and to help each other along as best we can. Mentorship alone, however, is insufficient, and it can be entirely too impersonal, too detached, too distant. We fall alarmingly short, as a community, in the development of friendships and intimacy, for as trans folk we have a strong inclination to be loners, to be lovers of solitude, to be islands unto ourselves. It is certainly here that we are called to reach out and to allow others to reach out to us that we may more easily build a loving, supportive, and diverse community.

To accept a friend as s/he is now and as s/he evolves means not imposing ones own will or expectations on the other, and means not judging the other. Though certainly it may well mean enjoying the daily discovery of new change and growth and evolution. C. S. Lewis suggested that one small part of what Jesus meant when he said that a thing will not really live till it first dies, is that it is no good to try to keep any of the thrills of a new relationship and it is no good trying to stifle change.[6] Better to let the thrill go and one will find a world of new thrills all the time. There is a certain evaporation of the relationship when the first blush of enthusiasm has gone, as when a couple returns from a honeymoon and begins to settle down. Yet, the interest continues on as the process of exploration and discovery, and the building of intimacy, reveals more and more treasures. Now this is of particular and obvious importance for us who are trans folk, for us, our companions, and loved ones often experience this dynamic of change most profoundly and most obviously in the discovery of our gender issues and in the evolution of our gender expressions and identities. Our call is

6. Lewis, *Christianity*, 99.

a complex one, in that we are called to witness to the evolution in ourselves as well as in others, as the dynamics of the relationship evolve and mirror the personal.

We tend to distrust intuition in favor of empirical knowledge and the scientific method, even in connection with our relationships and commitments to others, which become commodities to be measured and traded. The effect of this, however, is often that the relationships remain incomplete and flawed, for they continue to be handled as impersonal business transactions recorded on a balance sheet. In Luke's Gospel, Jesus is said to advise, "When you give a luncheon or a dinner, do not invite your friends . . . , in case they may invite you in return, and you would be repaid. But . . . invite the poor, the crippled, the lame, the blind. And you will be blessed because they cannot repay you" (Luke 14:12–14). Jesus calls us to recognize that relationships, that service to others, cannot be charted on a balance sheet. He calls us to see that relationships are built upon love and selfless service without any consideration of reciprocity. He calls us to a celebration of the realm of God in which there is cooperation and mutuality, rather than competition, commerce, and scorekeeping.

A teacher once said to me that there is nothing better than to keep silent. Perhaps we do not do much silent prayer, and sometimes periods of silence during public worship are often met with the same discomfort as a tasteless joke at a cocktail party. In the company of others, silence is most often an indicator of discomfort, awkwardness, tension, or even hostility. Only rarely is the silence of that kind that bespeaks profound comfort in mutuality. Now and then one has the experience of that very special kind of silence that accompanies familiarity, comfortable companionship, and love. For so many of us, the silence is unbearable, for it implies a kind of vulnerability, even nakedness. Only rarely does that silence serve as the hallmark of a kind of evolution, even a high-water mark, in a relationship with God, with another person, in a community, or even with oneself. It is that silence which speaks volumes and that says that the stories have all been told, that the social amenities have all been dispensed, that what is left is simply the being, the abiding, in each other's presence without conditions, without pretenses, without masks. It is living directly, vulnerably, and nakedly with the other.

In a world of alienation, isolation, rugged individualism, and chaos, we find our call is to build community and support each other. That is obvious. But more than that, we are called to examine and extend ourselves, to move beyond the trans community's ghetto, in order to begin for form or reform the personal relationships and commitments we have and need. We are called to continued change, and to affirm and embrace the continued change in ourselves and in those close to us. Like Jutta, we are called to be mentors, but also to be friends; to be "soul-friends," to work diligently day by day at building intimate and genuine relationships with each other and with God.

7

Courage

Homily given on August 8, 2004, at Dignity New York City
(Wisdom of Solomon 18:6–9; Psalm 33; Hebrews 11:1–19; Luke
12:32–48)

DO NOT BE AFRAID. These words, when they appear in Scripture,
are almost inevitably a sign of interesting things to come, intimated
by angels, or by God directly. They really mean that there is something to worry about, kind of like when a sales person says "trust
me." Moses had to confront Pharaoh, Joshua had Jericho, Gideon
had the Midianites. Mary, too, was told not to be afraid; yet she was
to be the mother of God and her heart was to be broken. "Be not
afraid" almost always means hang on, buckle your seat belt, for it is
going to be a rough ride. It also means, on a deeper level, that there
is a call to live thoroughly and intentionally.

Here the apostles are told to be not afraid, for they have been
given the kingdom of God. So often, our ideas about the realm of
God center around our dreams of justice, love, freedom, equality, and peace. For the disciples, gradually coming to realize that

indeed, as Andrew said, they had found the Messiah, their notions were similar, and included victory over their oppressors.

Yet Jesus, right after he talks about the realm of God, goes on to talk about giving it away—sell your belongings and give alms. He talks about being watchful, behaving as if the householder might return at any time; be like servants who await the employer's return from a wedding.

How strange. To inherit the kingdom of God is a frightening thing, for it is not at all like winning the lottery, or perhaps it is like winning the lottery, with the understanding that you had to give it all away. We are given the realm of God in order that we can give it away. Right before this, Luke records that beautiful passage about the lilies of the field, concluding with the line, "strive first for the kingdom of God and his righteousness, and all these things will be given to you as well" (Matthew 6:33). It is out of a discussion of priorities that Jesus begins to tell his disciples to trust him, but there is more. The other bookend to this passage is remarkable. Jesus says, "I came to bring fire to the earth, and how I wish it were already kindled. Do you think that I have come to bring peace to the earth? No, I tell you, but rather division" (Luke 12:49–51). Certainly, the prospect of giving away the gifts of the kingdom is alarming, and likely to give rise to arguments about the limits of charity.

Jesus's direction, to sell what you have and to give alms, is frightening. So frightening that we still argue about the limits of charity and generosity. Catherine de Hueck Doherty, author of the very popular book *Poustinia* and founder of Madonna House in Ontario, narrowly escaped death at the hands of the Bolsheviks in 1918 and made her way to North America. From an aristocratic family and with a natural gift for accumulating wealth, she had a series of personal revelations from which she developed her "little mandate," based on the stark words of Jesus, along with the practical theological view of St. Francis of Assisi.

> Arise—go! Sell all you possess.
> Give it directly, personally to the poor
> Take up My cross (their cross) and follow Me,

Going to the poor, being poor,
Being one of them, one of Me.
Little—be always little. . . . Simple, poor, childlike.[1]

Radical poverty. As you might guess, she was not always popular. As revolutionary as this seems, as unacceptably idealistic as this sounds, she has attracted hundreds of people—laity, clergy, and religious—to her, and she had gotten the attention of every pope since Pius XII. For her, living this "little mandate," working to build bridges among Christians, reaching out to the homeless, working against poverty, injustice, oppression, racism—all this amounted to what she felt was living authentically and thoroughly.

Where do we draw the line? To inherit the realm of God is to inherit the work of giving ourselves and our possessions for the life of the world. There is a fellow in Jenkintown, Pennsylvania, whose name is Zell Kravinsky, and over the last few years he has given away forty-five million dollars to charity. He gave away one of his kidneys to a complete stranger. He did the math and figured he would live just as well with only one, that his kids could give kidneys to one another if necessary, and that the odds of his developing kidney failure were so low, over against the certain odds of death for that stranger. For him, it was not a theological issue at all, but one of pragmatic ethics and math.[2]

In a classic argument, he offered two situations. In one, we see a baby drowning in a one-foot-deep puddle. Of course, we understand the immediate need to do something to save that life. In the other situation, we see photos of children starving in the Sudan or Afghanistan and we hesitate to send aid or money. For Kravinsky, the situations are absolutely equivalent and we must do good for those who are nearby as well as for strangers half a world away. Absolutely equivalent.

Most ethicists thought him mad. Of course, there is more to the story about organ donations and such. For us, the question is about this radical call to give. For us, it is not about math, but about being actual members of the body of Christ. We are called

1. Doherty, "Our Little Mandate."
2. Parker, "Gift."

to show uncommon hospitality to one another and to have faith in God. We are called to do good for one another and to be accountable for our words and acts, for when the householder returns, we will certainly be called to examine ourselves. The matter of reward and punishment for good or foul deeds almost immediately arises, for more often than not we ask, with the righteous Job, "Why do the evil prosper?" (Job 21:7). In the end, we are called to faith in God, despite all contrary evidence and persuasive argument.

In ancient Israel, it was commonly thought that the Messiah would come at Passover and so the brief portion from the book of Wisdom (18:6–9) quietly refers to that night in which the Israelites might have faith, once and again, in the salvation of the just. In the immediately preceding verse, the writer makes reference to the providential saving of the infant Moses and the Exodus, through whom and through whose faith many ascribe the very survival of the Jewish People. The section ends with praise of those who, supported by the joy and unity of faith, shared alike the same good things and dangers. That allusion to Passover is apropos too, for it serves to remind us of our organic unity with Christ established at the Passover meal with his friends, a meal we celebrate again each time we partake in the Eucharist.

The letter to the Hebrews, in some of the most beautiful and eloquent prose in Christian scripture, looks back on the faith of Abraham and Sarah. Their faith, which lay at the root of their covenant with God, finds itself, too, at the very origin of God's relationship with the Jewish people—showing once again how essential it is to have faith in what we cannot see. We too have a covenant with God. Baptized into the life, death, and resurrection of Christ, we are called into community to look after one another and to support the covenant relationship with God.

Be not afraid. What does it take, what does it mean, to look after one another when the other is the oppressor, is homophobic, transphobic, or a terrorist? What if the other is someone whose values are not ours?

We are not called to ignore or whitewash the issues that divide us. Jesus did not step back from confrontation. Rather we are called to look after one another, to engage personally with one another, and to live thoroughly, with all of ourselves. Giving a dollar to a homeless person, or a kidney to a stranger, or even forty-five million dollars to charity, will not change the world in any profound way. On the other hand it flies in the face of a materialist, impersonal society that says, with Rick in *Casablanca*, "It doesn't take much to see that the problems of three little people don't amount to a hill of beans in this crazy world."[3]

We are called to look at one another differently. By virtue of our being united with Christ, we are called to see as he sees and to behave accordingly. It is a frightening prospect, particularly because our understanding is so meager and changes so significantly from one generation to another, from one century to the next. Our problems are real and significant, of course, and we cannot play them down. We are each called to let go of fear, to get ready for an exciting ride, and to allow ourselves to live thoroughly.

3. Blaine, "I'm No Good."

8

Emmaus: A Call to Prophecy

THE TWO DISCIPLES ON the way to Emmaus as recorded in the book of Acts, Cleopas and his companion, had one of those moments. Their unexpected personal encounter with the risen Christ caused them to turn around completely, reverse course, retrace their steps, and return to Jerusalem—to danger. They moved from avoidance and fear to coherence, honesty, and courage.

Emmaus moments abound for all of us, religious or not, trans or not, for those who move consciously through life or not. There are so many ways of moving through life.

Some of us seem to move with circumstances, according to the prevailing winds of sentiment, opinion, and inclinations, finding ourselves in some place, a job, or a personal situation and not quite knowing exactly how we came to be there. A job offer here, a personal relationship there, a new apartment or home across town, all these seemingly minor circumstances seem to move us along like a feather on a spring breeze. Fate or necessity may propel us one way or another, almost unaware.

Others, perhaps fortunately, determine a direction for themselves at an early age, and with a single-mindedness, rationality, passion, and irresistible intensity, they succeed. At the end of twenty or thirty years, some are satisfied, while others are broken, disappointed, and confused, wondering why or how, in the midst of a midlife crisis.

Still others seem to respond to an inner voice or see to discern a direction amid the winds of culture, education, and family. Those who march to the beat of a different drummer sometimes seem to be the prophets and visionaries, while at other times seem merely peculiar, possessed, odd, or even a bit mad.

Many people, too, move along through any one or perhaps a combination of those three ways, according to the circumstances of their inner or outer life. And many will find further variations and alternatives in their pilgrimage, some of which present surprises, and they find that they are invited or driven to renewed introspection and self-evaluation. It is often at that midlife point, at which the perspective and priorities may alter in subtle or significant ways, that people find a new connection or a renewed connection with God.

Does God have a specific plan or vocation for each of us? That question is similar to whether there are soul mates with whom we are somehow destined to unite for lifelong (or perhaps eternal) happiness, joy, felicity, and prosperity. It is similar also to the idea that an individual may be destined somehow for a specific gender role, identity, or expression. There are those who would suggest that God does indeed predestine us for eternal joy, but that our free will and choices exist in order that we may cooperate voluntarily and eagerly with God's plan for us.

But can we know? Can we achieve a bit of certainty? Julian of Norwich, in the fourteenth century, proposed that we might bring a matter to prayer and then listen. If we truly listen, without expectations, it may be that we will hear nothing, or we may have a vague sense of hesitation, or we may have an impression that we are or are not on the right track. Just as important, of course, is rationality, for a sincere feeling of a call to a profession or course of action for which we have no aptitude may be worth reconsideration.

Can we know if we have got it right with, say, gender transition? Perhaps. Are we being carried along by peer pressure, depression, or daydreams, or are we responding to that inner compass? Is our internal conviction plausible and corroborated by a trusted confidante, or a medical or mental health professional? Some have a heart-stopping moment, an Emmaus moment, or a blinding flash of illumination, while others more gently come to an emerging realization, another sort of Emmaus moment.

These moments come in all sorts of ways and circumstances. For those of us who have roots in the Judeo-Christian tradition, we trust that these Emmaus moments are not only possible, but inevitable for those who pray and think, for those rooted in faith and reason.

For many people of trans experience, the central Emmaus moment is the realization of a core identity that moves an individual to the decision to enter the sacred space of gender transition, to affirm and embrace wholeness, honesty, and truth. Emmaus moments in trans lives virtually always involve an encounter with Divinity, one way or another, and they always call us to change. They extend in time and space to family, friends, neighbors, and coworkers. They bear elements of the prophetic vocation, calling all to reexamine their beliefs and convictions. Prophetic indeed, for it is the prophet, always the prophet, who calls us out of somnolence to activism and advocacy, out of comfort to energy. It is the prophet who brings wisdom and insight to bear in circumstances that are confusing, and it is the prophet who calls us all to repentance and justice.

Prophets are rarely predictable and while there were classes of prophets, such as those who followed Elijah and Elisha, there were also the unlikely and improbable (think of the prophet Amos, a shepherd and a dresser of sycamores), all of whom seem to have been selected by God to bring a specific sort of realization and message to God's holy and hopeful people.

As trans people have emerged from the shadows in ever increasing numbers, we may notice that the Holy Spirit dwells in this community just as securely and steadfastly as in the dominant culture, calling those in every generation to proclaim the truth of God's word to those who have ears to hear. A slogan on a sign outside a parish of the United Church of Christ says, "God is still speaking." The old message is simple enough, timeless, and radical, given to us over and over again: God is love and love casts out fear. For those in the LGBTQ community and in the dominant culture, the call is for inclusion and the affirmation of diversity within communities of faith. In our resistance to opposition and adversity at work, in academia, or in our own communities and families, we share in the prophetic vocation, for it is in this resistance that we proclaim the irresistible relentless truth of God's love. The prophetic vocation is both personal and corporate, in the same way that we are all members of the body of Christ, and particularly inasmuch as we participate in one another's struggles, defeats, and victories. As unlikely as any of us may be, simply by our presence we are meant to manifest the goodness of God and the presence of God.

The call that emerges for us from our various Emmaus moments is not only an individual call to truth within our own lives, but for us to proclaim the truth of God's goodness by our words and lives. Our call is to live truly, to live prophetically, proclaiming the radical, unconditional, infinite love by which we are called to live as children of God and heirs of God's realm.

9

Failure (Matthew 23:37; Luke 13:34)

I HAD A PROFESSOR in grad school who talked one day about his
son. His son was a gifted kid. His son, he told us, went to a school
for gifted kids, and somehow in spite of all they could do, his son
could not make it in college, and so joined the Navy. My professor
loved his son, but seemed crestfallen. This was not exactly what
he had planned for his son's life. A friend of mine mentioned recently that she is somewhat of a disappointment to her mother.
Her mom wanted so much to refer to "her son, the doctor," but my
friend's professional degree was not in medicine. To add to that
disappointment, she recently discovered that she was blessed not
with a son but with a trans daughter. This was not exactly what she
had planned.

Jesus had a very good idea of what it meant to fall short, to
fail, to have his motives questioned. On his way to Jerusalem, according to both Matthew and Luke, he notes that "it is impossible
for a prophet to be killed outside of Jerusalem"(Luke 13:33b). On
further reflection on the fate of all the prophets who had gone
before him, including his cousin John, called the forerunner, he
continues, "Jerusalem, Jerusalem, the city that kills the prophets
and stones those who are sent to it! How often have I desired to
gather your children together as a hen gathers her brood under

her wings, and you were not willing!" (Luke 13:34). Somehow, no matter how often God sends words of comfort and love and guidance to us, we manage to get it wrong, we lose our focus, and we go off in our own direction. One wonders if God honestly expects otherwise; God has, after all, created us.

One wonders if the Son of Man might have known all along that his plans would come to this, or if he had entertained the thought that this time it would be different. Jesus seemed, if not surprised, at least profoundly sad and upset when his love was thrown back in his face. "I have shown you many good works from the Father; for which of these are you going to stone me?" (John 10:32). He knew what it meant for those whom he loved to entirely miss the point, to entirely misunderstand and mistrust both his words and his works, and Jesus says, "If I am not doing the works of my Father, then do not believe me. But if I do them, even though you do not believe me, believe the works, that you may know and understand that the Father is in me and I am in the Father" (John 10:37–38). How well must Jesus understand our lives, our despair, and our grief when our motives are questioned, when the course of our very lives is subject to evaluation and criticism by those who have neither understanding nor empathy for our personal situations.

As a trans woman, I think I share some emotions and experiences with other trans people. Not the least of these is the peculiar nagging recurring sense that I am somehow more of a failure than others and sometimes simply on account of my being trans. There are things that I do or have done that have alienated people and I am possessed of an irrational habit of beating myself up over them. Mistakes that I made years ago return to my memory and contribute to my feelings of disappointment and regret. Rather like the prodigal son whose story is recounted in Luke's Gospel (15:11–32), I feel as if I have made a pretty good mess of my life. Then sometimes, it gets worse, as when the older brother comes in from the field and acts self-righteous. In some biblical commentaries, that older brother is supposed to be seen as self-centered and complacent, but in my imagination, I see him as entirely correct in his assessment of me. Like him, I come to see my life as a problem, and because I am a transgender. But unlike the prodigal child, I have not yet gone back to those whom I have offended to express my sorrow.

In the thirteenth psalm, David sings, "How long, O God? Will You forget me forever? How long will You hide Your face from me? How long must I bear pain in my soul, and have sorrow in my heart all day long?" (Ps 13:1–2). For many of us, it just seems to go on and on without letup, without end. So it must seem to God, as we all seem to go on and on in our blindness, poisoning our relationships, our religion, our governments, our environment, and even our future.

Over the centuries, we humans have wondered if we are truly made in the image and likeness of God; then, in some ways, God must certainly be like us, like you and me, while at the same time remaining "wholly other." In that prodigal child story, the father (is the son the only prodigal, not his father or brother?) is often taken to be an admittedly imperfect example of what Jesus wanted to tell us about God, that God is one who loves foolishly and un-conditionally, and not only that, but that as John said, "God is love" (1 John 4:8). Whatever love really means and however love really operates in the world to keep things more or less going on and on without us killing each other off or destroying everything, that is the central, life-giving spark that gives meaning to our under-standing of God. Yet, and perhaps *because* God is love, we find that a striking peculiarity of some forms or schools or traditions of Christianity is that it appears that God has failed and continues to fail. Over the course of what we sometimes still call salvation history, God confronts and continues to confront and continues to love a humanity that strayed, a people that strayed, and a human-ity that supported the crucifixion of God's son. God continues to love and to choose us, a group of people who missed, and miss, the point entirely, an all-too-human church that falls short—Peter who denied Christ, Judas who betrayed God's child.

Though God loves us, can we love ourselves? Augustine's line that "our hearts are restless until they rest in [God]"[1] is appropriate here, and Augustine's focus on restlessness points up one more dimension of our humanity. So many of us live with the most profound restlessness and dissatisfaction with our lives, we expect that we have a right to have perfection and so we find fault with people, things, circumstances, and ourselves. With our limited vision and abilities, we find fault with God as we understand and encounter God. At times God seems distant and indifferent and our experience is one of aridity, of dryness. All things are incomplete, all have fallen short, everything dies, and our thirst for stability, for change, and for final resolution is so strong that it hurts. If we understand it as a desire for and pursuit of God, then the very dissatisfaction we feel can be transformed into a prayer for union with God.

To encounter creation, to encounter ourselves and one another, is to encounter an unfinished project, a work in progress, and perhaps it is unfair to expect a tidy and flawless product this early. Johann Wolfgang von Goethe said that "life is the childhood of our immortality,"[2] and Jesus invited us to be as little children in our approach to life in general. As we think about the development of our lives, perhaps the call for us is not so much to look at failure or dissatisfaction or restlessness, but rather to play, to see what we can add to the projects facing us. Perhaps the call is to transform the energy of restlessness and dissatisfaction and to participate in the divine energy, in the life of God, by being cocreators, by cooperating in the evolution and development of the universe.

Can God really be like me? Imagine the tragic grief of the prodigal's father after his child went away. Imagine his pain when the angry and righteous brother refused to forgive. When Jesus was asked, how many times should someone forgive, he may very well have had this prodigal brother in mind when he said to forgive not seven times, but seventy times seven. Love, for Jesus, has no limit, no conditions, no end. Rather than ask whether God can be as exhausted, as tired, and persecuted as we think we are, we

1. Augustine, "Our Hearts."
2. Goethe, "Life."

might want to wonder how we ourselves might be more godlike. "You are gods, children of the Most High, all of you" (Ps 82:6) is what Jesus might remind us. This God in whom we live, move, and have our being, this very personal loving God, lives and moves in us and through us, in all the seasons and times of our lives. Before our broken, shattered dreams, in the face of our defeats, and in our triumphs, successes, insights, and *eureka* moments, this God is ever with us.

What is God for you? The task then becomes to square the idea of perfection with the idea of an exhausted, failing transgender God, a God who can suffer and who can understand our painful longings. It is in the largeness and greatness of God that we begin to see that God's love and compassion are central to the process of the interpenetration of human and divine and the consequent divinization of humanity.

One reason for Jesus's failure was that he was so much like them, like us. How boring to have a Messiah who is nothing more than a carpenter, with no political agenda, with no crown but that of martyrdom, with no zeal for the restoration of the political power and glory of Zion! Why bother with a Messiah who did nothing but a few healings, for there were many would-be Messiahs and many wonder-workers who healed as he did. Why bother with a Messiah who simply taught about love, who loved people for who they were instead of for what they did? Why bother with a Messiah who is simply there, loving and listening with compassion and understanding?

Jesus knew the frustration of misunderstanding, of plans gone awry. Jesus wept over Jerusalem, wept at Gethsemane (his view of what should happen vs. surrender to divinity). Jesus was misunderstood by the apostles, family, and authorities. In Mark's Gospel, he dies, not in glory, but in agony and anguish.

In the face of all that failure, shame, and regret, we continue to hope, we continue to strive, and we continue to struggle. What great comfort there is to see that God is with us, that Christ has experienced what we experience. We do not suffer alone. The suffering and failure is not the end of the story, though, and we are called to remember that on the third day, Jesus rose from the dead, trampling down death and upon those in the tombs bestowing life. Jesus rose from the dead and in his resurrection and triumph we rise from the ashes of our defeat and we rise in triumph.

10

Fear and Distrust

NEW YORKERS HAVE A reputation for being distrustful and cynical and like many of my fellow citizens, I think I know enough to be careful, to be a little fearful and skeptical when someone says those legendary words: "trust me." It is not necessarily that I dislike or distrust everyone, but I have a certain sensitivity to potential disasters, and I have what I conceive to be a healthy skepticism about the good will of people who find it necessary to warn me that I must trust them. I already tend to trust most people far too much, at least until they say "trust me." There is a plaque in my kitchen that says, "If you trust too much you may occasionally be deceived. However, you will live in torment if you cannot trust enough." In general, even if I am deceived, tomorrow is another day, and I can maybe recover from silly mistakes.

As trans people, we live with fear. We fear adversity in employment, housing, and health-care discrimination, as well as rejection and abandonment by family and friends. We fear the myriad forms of violence we are more than likely to face every day; we fear queer-bashing, we fear assault and mayhem, we fear discriminatory laws that seek to demean and devalue us, and we fear torture and even murder.[1] Many of us base our fears in our

1. The annual Trans Day of Remembrance is held in many localities

memories of childhood physical, sexual, and emotional abuse, while nearly all of us know someone who has been subjected to some form of oppression or physical abuse based on her or his expression of gender. We fear isolation and loneliness in life and we fear dying alone.

Fear can be one of our worst enemies. Fear is insidious because it arises out of our own consciousness, it can kill our self-esteem and deny our happiness. It can make us suspicious, cynical, self-centered, immobile, and full of self-pity. Fear can kill us moment by moment and put us in hell an inch at a time. It can prevent us from achieving spiritual maturity and true love. It can blind us to our own fundamental goodness, to our relationship with God, and to God's love and grace. Writing in the calamitous fourteenth century, at the very end of her book, Julian of Norwich identified four kinds of fear: fear of assault, fear of pain, doubtful fear which is a form of despair, and reverent fear. She goes on to suggest that the only good one of these is reverent fear.[2] The rest are crippling, blinding, paralyzing things which give a false view of life and of God. Notice that she did not say that they are unreal, or that we should not fear these things, for that would be irrational. These are indeed fearful and real and we need to come to terms with them as best we can.

Apropos of fear, oppression, and rejection, Luke concerns himself in the twelfth chapter of his Gospel with the phenomenon of opposition, the reality that Christ's teachings would meet with significant opposition, both among his faithful followers as well as others. Luke links a number of Jesus's sayings together to provide some measure of comfort and assurance to his followers, that they might be strengthened and have sufficient confidence to withstand the evil days to follow. Jesus says, "I tell you, my friends, do not fear those who kill the body, and after that can do nothing more. . . .

around the world on or about November 20 to commemorate the murders of the hundreds of trans people who are killed each year. See "Transgender Day of Remembrance" for information and a list of trans people worldwide whom we have lost.

2. Norwich, *Showings*, 25.

But even the hairs of your head are all counted. Do not be afraid" (Luke 12:4a, 7). Later Jesus says, "Do not worry about your life, what you will eat, or about your body, what you will wear. For life is more than food, and the body more than clothing" (Luke 12:22–23). He also says, "Do not be afraid, little flock, for it is your Father's good pleasure to give you the kingdom. . . . For where your treasure is, there your heart will be also" (Luke 12:32, 34).

"Fear not?" We find that admonition quite often in Scripture. Just before he asks Abram to leave the pleasant security of Ur in Chaldea, God tells him "fear not" and trust that God's plan for him included a vast array of descendants. Gabriel, just getting ready to spring the good news on Mary started out by telling her to "fear not." A clergy friend of mine said recently that this "fear not" line is kind of the biblical equivalent of "uh-oh," which portends or implies a number of things. It means something is getting ready to happen that I will probably not enjoy, but which will promote my spiritual growth and maturity, and which will ultimately resolve into a very, very good situation. It means that try as I might, I cannot evade or avoid this, and even if I were to succeed, the net result of that avoidance would be catastrophic. It means that I must change, I must submit to the will of God, I must accede to the eternal wisdom of the divine, and I must trust God.

Matthew, in his Gospel, talks about the same sort of opposition. He relates that Jesus, sitting on the Mount of Olives, said, "Then they will hand you over to be tortured and will put you to death, and you will be hated by all nations because of my name" (Matt 24:9). This warning should have come as no surprise, for Jesus told them when he called them, that they must "beware of them, for they will hand you over to councils and flog you in their synagogues; and you will be dragged before governors and kings because of me, as a testimony to them and the Gentiles" (Matt 10:17–18).

That line, "for my sake," nags quite a bit. The traditional view has it that it is Jesus's followers who do their work "for Jesus's sake," and it is for that reason they are persecuted. Certainly, during the first three centuries of Christianity, that view was entirely likely.

After the year 312, when Christianity became legal throughout the Roman Empire, that particular view lost some of its force (though admittedly, Christians have been persecuted simply by virtue of their Christianity many times throughout history). An alternative is to suggest that it is often the misguided followers of Jesus who do evil things for his sake. The (so-called Christian) heterosexist, patriarchal, socially conservative right often persecutes LGBTQ people, often commits outrageously evil and controversial acts, and use their fallacious understanding, their faulty interpretation of the gospel to justify their actions. We have all heard or read of the egregious criminal acts that these misguided people have committed in the name of religion, from the manipulation of the media and of legislation, to conspiracy, to assault and murder. It is an act of the most enormous hubris to use the gospel of God's eternal and boundless love and compassion to vindicate what is patently a flawed, inflexible, and loveless position, and to justify merciless and unpardonable acts of cruelty. Our task, mission, or calling here before this injustice is to a form of surrender, certainly, but it is not to traditional martyrdom. We must not go willingly to oblivion, to anonymity, to the stake, as did Felicitas and Perpetua, Serge and Bacchus. Our times are different, and we have (not much, admittedly, but some) legal and economic power. Rather, we are called to witness not with our blood but with the way we live our lives, with our votes, and with our voices. In the tradition of Ghandi and King, we are called to loving and nonviolent defense of our positions and our communities, using any legal and ethical means available.

John the Beloved disciple, writing many years later, recounts that Jesus said, "If the world hates you, be aware that it hated me before it hated you" (John 15:18). Also, he said, "They will put you out of the synagogues. Indeed, an hour is coming when those who kill you will think that by doing so they are offering worship to God" (John 16:2). We have much to fear, but we are called not to fear but to joy and peace, growing from the conviction, intimated in Luke's Gospel; that although the pain will not go away, we must be sure that pain is not and will never be the final thing, the last word. In her sixteenth revelation, Julian of Norwich recounts that God "did not say, You will not be troubled, you will not be belabored, you will not be disquieted; but God said, You will not be overcome. God wants us to pay attention to these words, and always to be strong in faithful trust."[3] The Gospel of John says it this way: "In the world you face persecution. But take courage; I have conquered the world!" (John 16:33b). Pain and death will not have the final victory. Always there is life and our goal must be to live in harmony with that God-given life, to attune with and synchronize ourselves with the rhythms and tempo and music of that life. Life is the gift of God, and that life we each enjoy expresses the light and love of God, the perfect love that casts out fear (see 1 John 4:18).

There is no question that Jesus knew our fears and strivings and pain. The accounts of his agony in Gethsemane and his sweating of blood speak more eloquently than we can of his intimate understanding of our human condition. Mark's Gospel underscores this very human reaction to pain and abandonment. Mark does not portray Jesus's passion and death as a glorification, as does John in his Gospel. Mark shows Jesus dying in agony and frustration and pain. Jesus cries out at about the ninth hour, "My God, my God, why have You forsaken me?" (Mark 15:34b) and a little while later, he "gave a loud cry, and breathed his last" (Mark 15:37). Even Jesus, in the face of incredible, devastating pain, seems to have doubted God's love. Even Jesus seems to have forgotten the words of the prophet Isaiah: "Fear not, for I am with you" (Isa 41:10a).

Almost everyone who suffers experiences this unspeakable sense of having been abandoned by God. In this glimpse of Jesus as a very human, very vulnerable, and very fragile person, we see a Messiah who is almost too much like us, almost too ordinary. It is a peculiarity of Christianity that our God can suffer, that Jesus, the Son of God, did indeed suffer with us, and suffers with us day by day, moment by moment. There is no doubt that Jesus experiences with us, suffers with us, lives with us, lives within and through us. In Matthew's Gospel, Jesus says, "When the Son of Man comes in

3. Norwich, *Showings*, 68.

61

glory, . . . the Father will say to those at the right hand, 'Come, . . . for I was hungry and you gave me food, I was thirsty and you gave me something to drink, I was a stranger and you welcomed me, I was naked and you clothed me, I was sick and you visited me, I was in prison and you visited me'" (Matt 25:31, 34b-36). Jesus knows how we hunger and thirst for justice, freedom, and peace in the face of runaway homophobia and transphobia. He knows how we feel naked and helpless and rejected by family, friends, employers, and neighbors. There are those among us who are languishing in prisons, unvisited, ignored, persecuted, and deprived of medical treatment. According to his own words, Jesus suffers with us, "as you did it to one of the least of these who are members of my family, you did it to me" (Matt 25:40). Jesus is there, just as much as he is here in this place, here in these words, here in the lives of all of us.

Not only that, but there is here the very pointed call to each of us to do something. For while Jesus is indeed with us in the daily struggles of our lives, he is at the same time calling us to a greater and more participative role in the salvation and support of people in our own community. As children of God, as a priestly people, we are called to minister to each other, not just in antiseptic, impersonal, spiritual ways, but directly. Jesus calls each of us and he calls us by name to do what we can to feed, clothe, visit, and love those who need us, just as if each one of them (and us) were (as in fact we all are) children of the living God. Liberation theology applies the radical message of the gospel to the radical inequalities and injustices of the world today. Here is that social gospel that some folks do not like to hear, for it calls us to be more than merely hearers of the word; it calls us to be doers of the word, to act on the word of God. We are called to work to soothe the pain and to help alleviate the fear of those who suffer in our community.

It is important to me that Jesus experienced suffering and it is important to me that there are others who can identify with my life experiences. That Jesus can know the frustrations and depression that I experience, that there are other transgender people who have walked and are walking the path I walk is a great comfort to me. It does not lessen the pain and frustration, but it provides a measure of security and peace to know that I am not entirely alone. More than that, it is a comfort to me to know that no matter how great it is, no matter that it seems that it will never end, I know that pain is never the final word. I know that those who have gone before me and Jesus who goes with me have survived. This gives me the courage and confidence that I too will survive.

In the face of spiritual aridity, of pain and suffering, and of abandonment, we must hear and heed the call to seek God. During the American Civil War, President Abraham Lincoln had frequent recourse to Ps 34 and there is a finger smudge in his Bible at the line, "I sought the Lord and He answered me, and delivered me from all my fears" (Ps 34:4).[4] As Lincoln must surely have felt, we are often as barren and dry after our prayers as we were before. We are called to trust, to trust that God does indeed hear our prayers and taste our tears, that God is with us, even and perhaps especially when we feel most alone, most barren, and most abandoned. For prayer unites the soul to God even when we feel we cannot, would not, or will not pray. In our prayer, in our pain, and in our fear, we are close to God and to each other, and in the solidarity of that experience, providing strong hands to comfort one another, we extend ourselves beyond ourselves and grow in such a way that we embrace and enfold one another, losing all sense of isolation and alienation.

4. pmarkrobb, "Permanent Mark."

11

Healing the Pain

TIME AND TIME AGAIN it happened. Jesus is on the way to do something and out of nowhere some needy person turns up and asks for help. "Jesus, Son of David, have mercy on us!" (Mark 10:47) or "Jesus, I am not worthy . . . but only say the word and my servant shall be healed" (Matt 8:8) or "If You had been here, my brother would not have died" (John 11:21).

In the face of the world's pain and heartbreak and devastation, Jesus walked among us healing, listening, loving, and teaching. "Go and tell John what you hear and see: the blind receive their sight, the lame walk, the lepers are cleansed, the deaf hear, the dead are raised, and the poor have good news brought to them. And blessed is anyone who takes no offense at me" (Matt 11:2–6). In the face of our pain, heartbreak, and devastation, Jesus comes among us, witnessing, honoring, and sharing our pain. "What do you want me to do for you?" is Christ's question. The question is not a simple one, for it demands that we *locate* our pain, and more, that we have some sense of what healing looks like.

Some of us will locate the pain within ourselves and having done that, we resist any move toward healing, seduced and imprisoned by the attention and pity of the crowd: "You are so very brave . . . you have overcome so much . . . how can you bear all this? . . . You, and people like you, are an abomination." Sometimes it is easier to be a transgender poster child, to bury our individuality and personality inside the label assigned by society. To give up our individuality and personality and to become a symbol is to distance ourselves from pain and suffering, from other people, and even from ourselves. To be a leper, an outcast, or a pariah is to be that kind of symbol—nameless, faceless, even voiceless. It is interesting that in only a very few instances, the person healed by Jesus is said to have followed him as a disciple. To rise above the pain and lay claim to individuality, knowing and believing in the personal love of a personal God, is a daunting and seemingly unattainable task for most of us.

Someone once asked me, "Suppose you were able to take a magic pill such that you would effortlessly blend in with the rest of society, such that you would never be 'clocked' as trans. Would you?" Quite honestly, I replied that I would not hesitate to forsake solidarity with the rest of the trans community, personal integrity, and total honesty for the gift of anonymity. That was close to twenty years ago. Now I am not so sure. See, this is a big part of who I am, and how I live, and how I interact with other people and with the world and with God.

Anonymity. In the seventh chapter of his Gospel, John relates that one year, during the Feast of Booths, Jesus did not go up to Jerusalem publicly with his disciples, but secretly, for his time had not yet come. This quest for anonymity was not about fading in and fading away, however. It had more to do with planning and preparing for the proper time and place for confrontation with a society and a system whose values and priorities were disordered. Teaching in the temple, Jesus called on the authorities, "Do not judge by appearances, but judge with right judgement" (John 7:24). For us too, the quest for anonymity ought not ever be focused on a perpetual obscurity; we must ever be mindful of our identities and our connections with each other. Our aim needs to be to transcend the unwelcome and the negative, and to turn our individuality to the service and love of truth, of God, and of each other.

Some of us will locate the pain within ourselves and will assume that it is associated with a personal sin or defect of character or will assume that the healing is needed only within the immediately and directly afflicted person. "Rabbi, who sinned, this man or his parents, that he was born blind?" (John 9:2). Sometimes the advantage to being a trans poster child has to do with being the center of attention, the squeaky wheel. Some of those suffering from demonic possession found themselves in the situation of being the center of attention. To overpower our surroundings with the force of our personality is to exert control over the immediate situation and to keep others at a safe and disempowered distance. In individual cases, Jesus took immediate and personal action. When confronting social injustice or institutional pathology, his approach varied. He cleansed the temple, expelling the money changers and throwing the place into an uproar. He healed on a Sabbath day in a synagogue, throwing the place into an uproar. He dared to enter Jerusalem on a donkey, accompanied by a small army of followers, and the whole city talked of nothing else.

Dying, he rose again and changed the whole course of history. Jesus saw clearly that whole institutions needed healing and at the ascension, he sent out his disciples to preach the good news of the realm of heaven to the ends of the earth. But what of us? Too often, don't we prefer to blame ourselves and situate the origin, life, and end of our pain within ourselves and our individual lives? It often seems better to isolate ourselves from the larger picture, better to avoid sharing the attention, and better to avoid confronting social pathology, injustice, and oppression.

For still others, the solution is to look to the environment, the memories, and the community for the roots of pain and for the etiology of the dis-ease. It is always so much easier to indict society for our individual ills, for by doing this we are able to distance ourselves from the situation; to be objective about it; and to rationalize, blame, explain, categorize, and classify. "It is society's fault," we say, "not the fault of any individual, but just one mark of an imperfect and human society. Actually, you know," we continue, trying to rationalize and be conciliatory, "it is nobody's fault. It is just the way things are." In this way too, we enable ourselves to take the role of a passive victim in need of rescue. When presented with the case of the woman caught in adultery, whose punishment would ordinarily be death by stoning, Jesus confronted and temporarily neutralized the social pathology, but he also made a point of confronting her about her history and role in the situation. Here is real objectivity for he did not seek to distance himself or her from the community, but simply and lovingly advised her to change the direction of her life. It is never all one or all the other; every disease, every painful situation, and every instance of injustice has many sides and can never be fully understood without a detailed, prayerful analysis. Healing must always involve the systems in which the individual is found.

Through my trans eyes, the world often seems less than hospitable. Hostility, mockery, fear, and ignorance all combine to meet the trans person as profoundly different, radically flawed, and threateningly evil. Stereotyping, when it happens, does not run along the lines of that associated with racial or sexual minorities; rather, it follows the pattern associated with disfiguring medical anomalies, psychological or developmental problems, and disease. Like the lepers and the demonically possessed in the gospel stories, transgender people are separated and ghettoized, underemployed, and rendered socially irrelevant. Some of us enter the sex industry as prostitutes, while others fade into a kind of obscurity and become the neighborhood oddities, not unlike a clown or the village idiot of a past generation. Sometimes the stereotyping and transphobia masquerades as admiration. Finding something to praise and minimizing the obvious differences in an attempt to neutralize an awkward situation is really no more helpful than assigning people to separate but equal schools, health care, public transportation, restaurants, or bathrooms. The difficulty is in enabling the society or office system to see through a clear lens that is neither convex nor concave. To be mocked and marginalized, certainly, is to develop an appreciation for the situation of the legions of poor and oppressed in the world, and it brings into clearer focus our fellowship with Jesus, enabling us to better understand his situation before Pilate and Herod.

It is profoundly in the *feeling with* or *feeling together* that we can as individuals and as a community begin to develop solidarity with each other apart from hierarchies and patriarchy. If God truly is love and loves personally, then God must also be compassionate, for love without compassion is at best mere impersonal theory. Without compassion we can remain stoic, detached, and rational, but once we enter into the pain with another, we can truly begin to love and be loved. Compassion is a leveler, it fosters a sense of equality between people, and brings urgency to the quest for justice. Once we enter into the pain of the world, we can truly appreciate its joys and beauty and begin to work with fervor and zeal for justice, freedom, healing, and peace.

It may be here that we find our call to heal. The call, though, is to heal the world through our presence in it and our love for it.

Healing, true healing of the soul and the memories, true healing of the world, must often begin with prayer and understanding, followed by forgiveness and reconciliation. Without these there remains a wall, crumbling and dangerous, preventing any approach, any healing touch, any loving embrace. Again Jesus says, "What do you want me to do for you?" Many of us, friends of Bill W. and others connected with the twelve steps, pray daily for the grace to "accept the things we cannot change, the strength to change the things we can, and the wisdom to know the difference." In the realm of healing as it presents itself for our consideration as transgender people, this prayer is magnificent in its straightforward statement of the question, and we can do no more than to commend it for continued meditation. Let us all pray for the gifts of faith, hope, compassion, and wisdom.

12

Ockham's Razor

ALTHOUGH THE IDEA PROBABLY originated with Durand de Saint-Pourcain, and was invoked not only by William of Ockham but also by Nicole d'Oresme and Galileo, the clearest and most common articulation was certainly that of Ockham, a fourteenth-century Franciscan friar, the philosopher and political theorist known as *Venerabilis Inceptor* (the Venerable Beginner) and *Doctor Invincibilis* (Invincible Doctor). The idea is at the root of nominalism, the philosophical school of thought that denies the universal concepts such as "mother" have any reality apart from the individual things signified by the universal or general term. (Thus, it may be seen to run utterly contrary to the notion that universals exist and are known through particularity.) Most commonly, the idea, which is also known as the "law of economy," or the "law of parsimony," is that *non sunt multiplicanda entia praeter necessitatem*, or that plurality should not be assumed, that entities are not to be multiplied without or beyond necessity. Said more simply and considerably less precisely, "if it ain't broke, don't fix it," and "simplicity is goodness."[1]

What has all that got to do with being transgender? Well, maybe nothing really, but then again, maybe a lot. For the moment,

1. "William of Ockham's Nominalism."

treat it as if it were a potentially important footnote. Keep it lightly in mind, as we will return to these notions periodically during this discussion. You see, Ockham invites us to reconsider the notion that the categories we have generated have any basis. Over time we have discerned and described more and more categories of distinction within our community and then, having defined them, we have begun to behave as if these categories have a true basis in actuality.

Look at a rainbow and then look at the crayon drawing of a rainbow you did in first grade. The natural rainbow's colors kind of blend one into another without you really noticing, while the crayon depiction shows a more immediate switch from one color to the next. Think of Toulouse-Lautrec's poster style and contrast it to reality. Similarly, with our categories, we have sought to define and limit the parameters of our experience and expression to make order and develop understanding. However, what we have ended up with is only an approximation of what truly is because the universal concepts have no real existence.

The damage occurs when we begin to make these artificially constructed categories the basis of our social interchanges, friendships and associations, political agendas, and educational activities. The damage occurs when we assume that these categories and distinctions we have made are universals, that they are clear and mutually exclusive, and that somehow they reflect some qualitative aspect of being. The damage occurs when we begin to rank-order people based on an appraisal of relative worth, grounded in association with or approximation of these categories. Philosophy really can, and often does, have a profound influence on people's lives because the way we explain how we see and understand reality impacts, consciously or unconsciously, every waking moment.

What we need to do is recognize that generating complex theories does not make our lives easier. Nor does the development of lists and the discernment of categories. Umberto Eco voices a common idea of the late classical and early medieval period, when one of the characters in his novel *The Name of the Rose* is heard to observe that there is nothing more wonderful than a list.[2] It was this very movement toward the multiplication of categories, toward unnecessary complexity, that Ockham attacked. His severe passion for logic dictated the absolute necessity to distinguish between the essential and the incidental, between knowledge and belief, between fact and conjecture.

Our community these past many years has seen the development of a degree of complexity which approaches being Byzantine. It may indeed be helpful to note the shades of variety that mark the lives and lifestyles of our people and it may be interesting and instructive to take note of trends, cycles, patterns, and other indicators of commonality. We must not, however, fall into the trap of presuming that these indicators have reference to pre-existing natural categories that have themselves any actual existence. *Post hoc* cannot be held to demonstrate *propter hoc*—just because one thing follows another, one cannot presume that the first caused the second and for that matter, one cannot even presume that the first really exists.

Within our present structure there are two opposing forces at work, and as a community we are trying to accommodate both of them. One force is toward the notion that we are one community, that we must work to strengthen the community, and that we are to build bridges between and among individuals within the community, segments of the community, and other communities. The other force is toward the idea that we are a set of categories with very little of substance to bind us together, save for our common oppression at the hands of those who control the dominant culture, who in their ignorance see us as cut of the same cloth. That force which is toward unity and building bridges tends to see the erection of categories and divisions as separatist and destructive of what is still a fragile community, while that force which is oriented toward the precise definition of sets and categories suspects others of a lack of respect for the special needs of those who associate primarily with specific groups.

2. Eco, *Rose*, 983.

Both, of course, are wrong, for the notion of a transgender community is just as much an artificially-constructed category as is the notion of any smaller subcategory. Wrong because it is too easy to act as if the categories are actually there and that they are permanent, immutable, and exclusive. Wrong because all the words do little except describe ways of living, thinking, and relating to others. Wrong because the categories do not talk about any essential quality by which a true state of being might be described.

Our choice of words and our grammar often can subtly imply that we are describing static states of being. There is a profound difference between describing someone as a woman or man of transgender experience and describing her or him as a transgender man or woman. The first acknowledges the personal, accidental, or incidental nature of the experience (which is all we can really know), while the second posits that there is an essential universal category of humanity being described (an unnecessary conjecture which can neither be proved nor disproved). Moreover, and more fundamentally, each one presumes that the categories woman and man have actual, essential existence.

The apparent tension between these two positions is similar to that between the ontological theories of Heraclitus and Parmenides. Heraclitus focused on the here and now, on what he saw, and proposed that nothing is stationary, that everything is in a state of flux, constantly becoming something else, renewing itself. Without that motion and change, we could know nothing. The implication is that there are no real, essential categories, because stability cannot be assumed. Parmenides, however, reached behind reality to a fundamental if ineffable actuality. He moved away from that which could be empirically verified and looked to another level of existence, a higher one, to explain the cycles, patterns, and vicissitudes of life. He proposed that there might be a kind of essential eternal actuality that does not change, which has always existed and will always exist.

Centuries later, Ockham seems to have followed in the footsteps of Heraclitus when he suggested that we must take care to distinguish between what we know and what we believe, because it is likely that what we know is sufficient to explain observed phenomena and the addition of belief or conjecture may complicate our epistemology unnecessarily. The simpler answer, or theory, has a much greater likelihood of being correct than the more complex. Simplicity is obscured and we complicate our lives when we confuse unity with conformity, and instead of celebrating our spectrum of differences, we let them divide us. Though every rainbow is different, there is still in each instance but one multicolored rainbow, not a dozen monochromatic rainbows.

Charles Peguy observed that a "great philosophy is not that which passes final judgment, which takes a seat in final truth. It is that which introduces uneasiness, which opens the door to commotion . . . [and which is] without fear."[3] What we must do now is to explore ways of understanding and defining our realities, not necessarily with a view of maintaining the status quo or of discovering or articulating some kind of final, irrefutable, immutable truth. The endeavor has rather to do with introducing uneasiness and of discovering a way of thinking which works here and now, in simplicity. As time passes we find it necessary, for example, to develop and rearticulate our understanding of God. It is not the case that God changes, but rather that humanity, society, and civilization change, and so it becomes necessary for every new generation to express its understanding of God in accordance with its own vision, just as it is necessary to reinterpret the idea and experience of God anew for every generation. So too with our community's articulation of itself, we must redefine and reenvision ourselves and our community anew with each new generation of trans people.

Still, there are those who long for complexity and obscurity, for multiplication of categories, and for exclusivity and divisions. The disastrous consequences now present themselves as infighting, horizontal hostility, and intolerance. On one level, of course, the notion that categories and states actually exist and are stable can provide a measure of comfort to someone just emerging in our community. Such a notion may provide a certain sort of strength to the community as it emerges and achieves greater and greater

3. Peguy, *Verities*, 120.

self-awareness, autonomy, and confidence. On the other hand, individual people and groups soon become enmeshed in the rhetoric and are persuaded to accept a view of a stable world. The pattern by which we oppress each other is strengthened. Although the dominant culture is gradually becoming more open to new ways of viewing our (and their) lives and lifestyles, the tendency is now to see, to insist upon, and to restrict the options to only three or five colors, for example, when considering sexual orientation or gender identification. Remember that first-grade drawing of a rainbow mentioned earlier and how real rainbows are simultaneously simpler and more magnificent?

The unfortunate tendency is to ignore change, which is the only constant thing, the only real thing, in the universe. In our lives and in our lifestyles, we symbolize and embody change and just as change is resisted, feared, and even rejected outright (for entropy, it seems, is always preferred), so are we resisted, feared, and rejected. Furthermore, as we evolve and change in our expression and articulation of ourselves and our community, so do we find the very same resistance, fear, and rejection within our very community. Too often we make ourselves miserable trying to conform to others' expectations, trying to refuse to change (as if that were possible), trying to freeze time, and trying to make other people comfortable with us, as if we were somehow guilty or deficient. And our oppression at the hands of the dominant culture continues.

Unity is indeed in community, but that unity cannot be based in artificially constructed categories, but rather in respect for diversity of races, cultures, and talents. And diversity is a great and wonderful gift. It is not served by setting up distinctions based on social or economic advantage, physical status, or surgical experience. Secret handshakes and rites of initiation or passage do not make a community. They may, however, witness to a community that already exists on its own. There are too few of us and far too much oppression; we cannot afford to oppress each other. We cannot permit ourselves or others to use artificially constructed categories to divide us, for we are all transgender people, all of us fundamentally equal. How we achieve or arrive at that self-definition is irrelevant. While the nuances and distinctions within categories may be interesting, even they are superfluous and subject to change. Remember, entities ought not be multiplied beyond necessity and simplicity is goodness. People are who and what they are, and we all have the right to define and enjoy or change our lives, our situations, and our social milieu without answering to anyone else. We cannot allow status and class to divide us.

We can retain our conscious awareness of how we use language to manipulate our reality and understanding, and develop ways of building community, understanding that community, too, is an artificially constructed concept, subject to change. We can intentionally and purposefully develop a concept of a unified community, in which each of us has the unencumbered right to make decisions about her or his own life, in which each of us is considered and heard, irrespective of membership in or association with any other artificially conceived categories.

Some have noted with interest and anticipation that we seem to be on the verge of something, that this decade is, in truth, our decade. We are moving beyond a slightly myopic consciousness of the trans community to the larger and more distant issues of the construction of gender and social roles, and to the matter of gender oppression. At the same time, we are moving from feeling victimized and helpless to feeling empowered. By extension, from empowerment we are coming to realize that we must, as a community, take positive action on our own behalf. We are coming to realize that as we develop and evolve, we have the obligation to work to oppose and to overcome gender-based hatred, fear, intolerance, bigotry, and oppression.

It is no longer simply to focus on ability and empowerment, but rather what is emerging is our obligation to take specific and positive actions on our own behalf. The further implications of this have to do with our projection of future events, with the empowerment of individuals, and with our abilities to transcend these artificial categories. It is now well within our power to understand and envision that which is greater than or beyond our present reality.

We are witnessing unprecedented, profoundly positive changes in the attitudes and priorities of the community. As time's apparent velocity accelerates, the connection between our present state and the immediate future is clearer and we are seeing clearly that our future is within our control. More importantly, we are witnessing the birth and evolution of significant and widespread political activity and that political activity is quickly becoming a centerpiece in our community's life and work.

13

Relationships: Human and Divine

THREE THOUSAND YEARS AGO at Shechem, Joshua conducted a tremendously important ceremony of reconciliation and covenanting (Josh 24:1–28). It seems that there were some Israelites who remained in Palestine while the rest were sojourning in Egypt. Both groups worshipped the one true God, the God of Abraham, Isaac, and Jacob. For forty years, though, the Egyptian Israelites also had the Mosaic law, the Ten Commandments, the Passover, and the name of God. Who would have anticipated the outcome of their decision to follow Moses and Aaron? Who could have foretold their decision to take Joseph's bones and return to Canaan? They brought with them the memories of oppression, starvation, the plagues, the Exodus, and the years of wandering in the desert. Now, Aaron, Miriam, and Moses are dead. Joshua, the son of Nun, is the appointed leader and successor of Moses. In this passage, we have the remnants of the very necessary ceremony of reunification, as well as the ceremony of rededication of the Israelites to God according to the Mosaic covenant. There is a powerful and moving litany or dramatic chorus between Joshua and the people, and finally the covenant is renewed and a memorial stone is erected. Very much in the tradition of the covenants made by God with Noah, Abraham, and Moses, this covenant is accompanied by high drama, a sacrifice, and a crowd of people. There is an active choice on the part of all the people of the twelve tribes to enter into a covenant with God. They could not have had any idea of the consequences of this choice.

Two thousand years ago in Palestine, Jesus—another Joshua—walked among us and spoke to us about what a relationship with God, our heavenly parent, might look like and could involve, and Jesus told us what it would mean to follow him. Toward the end of the sixth chapter of John's Gospel, a number of people stopped following Jesus after they heard some particularly difficult teaching. He turned to the Twelve and asked, "Do you also wish to go away?" One of them, Simon Peter, responded, "Lord, to whom can we go? You have the words of eternal life" (John 6:67–68). As John said in the first chapter of the same Gospel, Jesus is the Word of life, coeternal with the Creator (John 1:1). The twelve had been following Jesus for about three years and could never have envisioned the consequences of responding to his invitation to "follow me and I will make you fish for people" (Mark 1:17). Though not nearly as dramatic as the interchange between Joshua, the son of Nun, and the Israelites at Shechem, the covenant is nonetheless sealed by an active choice on the part of the Twelve to continue to follow Jesus. Could they have had any idea of the consequences of this choice?

Words and deeds are often in conflict. Joshua's covenant was eventually broken. In the same way, Noah's covenant was broken, Abraham's covenant was broken, Moses's covenant was broken. Again and again we rebelled, and continue to rebel, against the Most High, citing God's failure to meet our expectations, citing our infinite human potential for the perfection of the world. Again and again we return to God like the prodigal son, hoping to make a deal and make things right again. Peter denied Jesus three times. Judas betrayed Jesus. Everyone fled, but many returned. Schism and heresy divide people from each other and from the church. Angry people curse God and forsake their covenant relationship with God.

The decision made in Egypt by the Israelites to follow the Almighty God, the decision made by the Twelve to follow Jesus the Child of God, is made for most of us at our baptism, well before we know what is going on, much less have any understanding of the consequences of such a decision. But it is reaffirmed as we come together, week by week, continuing in the apostolic tradition of the prayers and the breaking of bread. As we join together to speak the words of the Creed, the Symbol of Faith, we continue to affirm that decision to be one people, the people of God, joined to God in a new covenant relationship grounded in love, honesty, and simplicity.

The implications of this decision are not simple. By choosing to follow God, we are not merely choosing to attend church from time to time and be a more or less decent person. It involves more than the self-evident principle of natural law, to do good and avoid evil, and it involves more than the following of all the commandments of the Mosaic law, or even the minimal details of Noah's covenant. During the course of Jesus's ministry among us, he gave us some idea of his vision of covenant in the two great commandments, to love God with our whole heart, soul, and mind, and to love our neighbor as we love ourselves. He talked about the practical application of these as well: heal the sick, clothe the naked, comfort the sorrowful, feed the hungry, and visit prisoners. We are called to proclaim the good news of salvation to all the nations, even to the ends of the earth. We are to continue in the apostles' teaching, the breaking of bread, and the prayers. In all the changes and transitions of our lives, we are to love God and we are to love one another.

The religious element is part of what characterizes the truly human. Do you remember Zacchaeus, the tax collector (Luke 19:1–10)? Jesus praised him lavishly, because Zacchaeus did his best, in a personal, practical, and loving way, to deal honestly with his fellow men and women. In addition to good words, faith, and almsgiving, he had committed himself to good actions. It is often the interpenetration of the spheres that alarms people. In the late 1960s, many people were astounded and seriously distressed when clergy left the security and regularity of their traditional roles in order to meet people as equals and on their own terms. Liberation theology developed and still more people were alarmed and retreated into a nostalgic kind of neoorthodoxy and rigid traditionalism.

Jesus advised us to be like little children and one of the characteristics of children is simplicity. They have the good sense to avoid trying to separate the parts of their lives into boxes. For them, church, school, and play are all similar, with many of the same people and many of the same rules. In the third chapter of Genesis, the chronicler relates that it was at the moment of disobedience that adults lost the childlike understanding that all things, all places, and all situations are fundamentally, profoundly alike. It was at the moment of turning from God that we adults began to use our new wisdom to make distinctions and divisions. Rather than follow God's leadership, we adults develop complex categories and special rules for special situations.

We often separate our medical and personal histories, our education, our work, and even our family life from the rest of our lives, from our relationship with God, and from other people, with the concomitant result that we are haunted by a sense of being "othered" and of profound alienation even from ourselves. We adults isolate religion and God from our "real" lives, and then blame God for our feelings of isolation and alienation, and finally claim that God and religion have lost their relevance and meaning. It may make life feel simpler, in a way, to keep religion, spirituality, and God separate from our daily lives in the "real world," but it can lead to a vague, persistent sense of unease, emptiness, and spiritual aridity, unrelieved by whatever incidental traditions or orthodoxies we may embrace.

In *This Hebrew Lord*, John Spong examines the loneliness experienced by Christ—the loneliness of being who you are in a world that does not understand.[1] We all know that loneliness, so often misunderstood, miscommunicated, misrepresented, alienated, and suffering in silence at the hands of those who cannot

1. Spong, *Hebrew Lord*.

or will not understand us. Jesus knew just who he was, but we humans demanded to remake him according to our own needs and dreams. He was to be our military general, our ruler, our god of vengeance, our wonder-worker, our defender of every aspect of the law and holy tradition. He was to be a god made in our image and likeness. He was to be our slave. Yet in perfect simplicity, freedom, and love, he rejected conventional piety and legalism, turned away from irrelevant categories, and embraced lepers, foreigners, women, and even the dead. In Jesus and in his life among us, we see the commingling of the divine with the human, the sacred with the secular. In him we see the living out of the Trinitarian love of God's self-love and the love of God for all of created reality, without difference or distinction. In Christ we begin to see the face of the loving God in whom we live, move, and have our being.

Truly, the religious element is what characterizes the truly human. We cannot be fully, truly human till we reverse our inclination to isolate the various aspects of our lives. By renewing our covenant with God, by living in cooperation with God and the universe, we can overcome the malaise of the so-called post-Christian era, the sense of loneliness and abandonment. By endeavoring to unify our lives, to be at one with God, we can achieve a sense of reintegration and well-being; we will find that there is real meaning and value in our lives. Another Joshua, this one the central figure in a series of parables by Joseph Girzone, brings this message to the attention of a growing number of contemporary readers. In the first novel, *Joshua: A Parable for Today,* Girzone says that the heart is the source of true religion, and that religion is the free expression of love for and relationship with God, intended to generate peace and joy within us.[2]

Getting back to Joshua and the return and reunification of the Israelites in their ancestral homeland, our call is also to return, to return to our birthright as children of God. Our call is to open all the doors and to bring ourselves—every aspect of ourselves—to God and to invite God to enter in and be with us through all the seasons of our lives. There is more to this, however. There is the

2. Girzone, *Joshua,* 264.

recognition that we can in no way anticipate or envision all the consequences of our choices. The decision to follow Christ will always be irrational, for rationality is but a noble human attempt to make sense of a divine reality that will always be beyond our ken. The decision to follow Christ must finally be an act of intuition, a gift of faith for each of us. Jesus says, "No one who puts a hand to the plough and looks back is fit for the kingdom of God" (Luke 9:62). It is Christ who calls each of us by name. We are called to believe the call and to respond.

14

Resurrection and Eternity (Matthew 22:23–40)

IN A POPULAR TRAVEL guide written in the middle ages, Sir John de Mandeville described for his readers the wonderful things people might see if they traveled as widely as he.[1] In the lands of Ethiopia, for example, there was a race of people with only one foot, which was enormous, and was used primarily to shield them from the intense heat of the sun. Elsewhere, perhaps it was in "Prester John's Land," or the lands beyond India, there were people whose heads were not above, but rather below, their shoulders.

Five hundred years ago, Spanish explorers came to Florida in search of a miraculous fountain, whose waters were reputed to be capable of giving eternal youth to anyone who drank or bathed in them. Those same explorers sought to find their way to the land of El Dorado—a place where the supply of pure, fine gold was unlimited. A century and a half ago, some of our ancestors came to America expecting to find streets paved with gold in this land of opportunity.

It is interesting what people will believe about far-away places. Do you ever wonder what heaven will be like? When I was in

---

1. Mandeville, *Travels.*

third or fourth grade, Sister said that dying was like falling asleep, and that we would then wake up in heaven. We would all enjoy perfect health and we would all be exactly thirty-three years old, because it was the perfect age, the age at which Jesus was crucified, died, and rose from the dead . . . and that way we would all be like Christ. None of us thought then to question the reliability of her intelligence sources or to wonder how exactly she knew that, of course, but we rather liked the idea that somehow, our good intentions, works, and our faithfulness would be rewarded. At the time, though, for a room full of nine-year-olds, thirty-three seemed really old and far from perfect, and we were mystified, for who would ever want to be *that* old? Furthermore, if everybody was going to be thirty-three, how would we relate to our parents and grandparents, aunts, and uncles? Would they still even be our parents and grandparents, aunts, and uncles?

Today, by contrast, thirty-three sounds pretty good to me, even though there have been some major changes in my life since I was that age. If I could be thirty-three again and lose a few pounds, that would make for a really attractive situation, all other things considered.

This story of the seven brothers in the books of the Maccabees provides us with an insightful look at the zeal and faith of the Jewish people during the horrific reign of Antiochus Epiphanes, who sought to eradicate all traces of Jewish culture and religion, with a view to subsuming them into a single culture. By forcing this small, troublesome people to renounce their religion, their God, and their way of life, it was thought that they would be more docile and therefore significantly easier to govern.

But this small, troublesome people refused to be destroyed, refused to renounce their unique identity and relationship with God. It was clear that their national existence was at an end along with their lives, and as we read here, one of the brothers spoke up in defense of their faithfulness to tradition and the law of their ancestors. Significantly, as he died, he affirmed his faith that God would raise them up to live again for ever. The third brother, too, affirmed his faith that in the resurrection, he would receive back not just his life, but also his hands and his tongue. The fourth brother, likewise, affirms his faith that God will raise them up in a resurrection to life.

The idea of resurrection for the just was a relatively late development, involving not merely a resuscitation of the earthly body and a continuity of the present life, but, you might say, a transformation or translation into an entirely new mode of existence. In the words of these brothers we hear the faith of those who have been nourished from their infancy by the words and traditions of their people. We hear the faith of the psalmist, who confidently pleaded for God's help—"I call on You, for You will answer me, O God; incline Your ear to me and hear my words" (Ps 17:6). In the same psalm, the psalmist says, "when I awake, I shall be satisfied, beholding your likeness" (Ps 17:15b). We hear the confidence and joy that they—and we—are the apple of God's eye, hidden in the shadow of God's wings, and that on waking, they—and we—shall be content in God's presence.

This calls us, certainly, to give some thought to what we believe. In the Apostles' Creed, we affirm our faith in the resurrection of the body and life everlasting, but how easy and tempting it is, for many of us understand the Creed merely as a symbolic or metaphorical reality, or perhaps as the vestiges of an old folk tale, no more relevant to modern life than Mandeville's *Travels* or the search for El Dorado.

There are some modern writers who would propose that all such ideas are merely primitive interpretations or tropes of self-evident ethical principles. They suggest that a new rational Christianity will soon emerge—a reconstructed, modern Christianity without resurrection, miracles, sin, sacraments, forgiveness, or the transforming power of conversion and deification—to speak to the needs and experience of modern people. In this new view, Christianity, purged of its unique characteristics, is nothing more than one among many absolutely equivalent ethical systems that urge us to do good and avoid evil. They propose that the reward of good works is in the doing of the good works themselves and in social approbation.

Now here, in the twenty second chapter of Matthew's Gospel, some scholars propose the question directly to Jesus (Matt 22:23–27). These scholars, from the Sadducee party, tend to have a very conservative, fundamentalist opinion about divine revelation in that they believe it may be found only in the Torah. They deny resurrection, immortality, retribution in a future life, and angels, and they tend to be more interested in politics than in religion.

When they pose the question, they want to test Jesus and see what he is made of—they want to see what Jesus believes about resurrection, and his very interesting answer is in two parts. First, he demonstrates that there really is such a thing as a silly question. Clearly, in the resurrection, people can no longer die and there is no need for procreation in heaven. The question about the hypothetical seven brothers is frivolous on that level. That is not the end of it though, for we wonder, as his listeners must have wondered, what will become of relationships that have been formed here in this present life. Our characters and personalities are formed in the crucible of relationship and for many people, the continuation and perfection of the course of our life would seem to be both logical and just. It might mean the continuation of a loving relationship or the achievement of justice, freedom, and peace, or a life of intimacy with God.

In the final analysis, we do not know. Jesus does not say. That people neither die nor are given in marriage certainly does not invalidate the relationships that begin here. Certainly, the beauty and holiness of our relationships as LGBTQ people of faith can never be denied, though there are many today in the church and in government who would deny our right to equality, who would deny our spirituality, who would deny the reality of our lives in Christ. They would make the matter of our right to equal rights a litmus test of patriotism and religious orthodoxy.

In the resurrection, we cannot know what to expect, for the current state of our knowledge and understanding does not provide us with a vocabulary or context in which to understand what we have not yet experienced. What we see in this gospel is that it is a mistake to begin from our experience here, for no comparison is possible.

The second part of his answer reopens and restates the question, by bringing the reference back to the Torah. He takes the question out of the context of their—and our—limited understanding, out of the context of theology and a conversation about the resurrection. While holding on to the Torah, he moves the question into the realm of philosophy and logic, and a consideration of the Hellenistic gentile concept of immortality. That we may expect to enjoy immortality has nothing to do with us, our actions, and our thoughts, and everything to do with the nature of God, who is revealed in Scripture as the God of Abraham, Isaac, and Jacob. God is the God of the living, who enters into personal, intimate relationship in history with us and loves us with an everlasting love, a love stronger than death. Jesus reminds them—and us—that it is inconceivable that God could love in an imperfect and transient way. Immortality focuses on the essential things of life—covenant relationships and God's perfect love.

If we believe in God, then we may feel called to trust God and place ourselves in God's hands for a future that could not possibly exist. To deny the resurrection is to deny that Jesus himself rose from the dead, to deny the uniqueness of the gospel, and it is to place God among the statues in the Metropolitan Museum of Art or among the ethical teachers of non-Christian faith traditions.

In this gospel we are called to consider what is really essential. Whether the resurrection takes place in the Hebraic terms described by Paul—white garments and getting your body and soul reunited—is not clear. Sister may have been right, too, about perfect health and being thirty-three years old, but that is not clear either. Jesus calls us in this gospel to see resurrection not as a continuation of our present life but as a fulfillment, not only of our individual lives, but of life itself. He calls us to consider the personal relationship we have—individually and as a holy people—with God, and to realize that in the end we are not in charge. We are called not to be God, but to be God's people, enjoying God's eternal, undying love for us played out uniquely in God's incarnation among us. In seeing the affirming and life-giving nature of that relationship, we should enjoy the loving relationships we have with one another here and now, for in them we experience something of the love God has for us.

Admittedly, that is not easy. We live in an increasingly materialistic culture, in which we are called to have self-reliance and faith in wealth-management services. Faith in God is more than an intellectual exercise, and there are those in our own LGBTQ community who would deny the relevance of Christianity in an increasingly savage and homophobic world. There are those, too, who would deny the relevance of an increasingly homophobic and transphobic church.

In some way, it comes to trust. If the issue remains an intellectual puzzle, then it may be quaint and interesting, like Mandeville's *Travels*, but it is not about faith. Our society does odd things with faith though. The media makes much about the various rabidly evangelical Christians, militant Muslims, sexually irresponsible clergy of all faiths, and homophobic Catholic and Orthodox prelates. In doing this they manage to paint all people of faith with the same broad brush, and quietly devalue us all, undermining the good we accomplish and the ideals we hold. If we are not vigilant and courageous in maintaining our faith, if we do not support one another, in time it will be easier to forsake our faith than to maintain it. In the end, as Paul counsels the Thessalonians (see 1 Thess 5:12–22), we must turn back to the relationships we have here and now, in this present life.

Brothers and sisters, we must pray for one another and with one another. Let us pray that we may be delivered from confused and evil people and ideas; for, as Paul says, not everyone has faith. Let us pray for an increase of faith, compassion, sanity, and charity for ourselves and for the church and let us pray that sincere people of faith may be delivered from degradation and oppression. In our relationships and in this community, we are the hands and heart of God, helping and loving one another as Christ loves us. Let us pray for discernment to hear God's word to us and for the wisdom, strength, and courage to respond with eagerness and faith.

15

Shame on You! (Mark 12:28–34; Matthew 22:34–40; Luke 10:25–28)

MATTHEW AND LUKE AGREE that it was a lawyer that asked the question and both of them agree with Mark about the answer. The whole thing ends up becoming the basis for ethical behavior under the new covenant. As Luke tells the story, the lawyer asked, "'Teacher, what must I do to inherit eternal life?' He said to him, 'What is written in the law? What do you read there?' He answered, 'You shall love the Lord your God with all your heart, and with all your soul, and with all your strength, and with all your mind, and your neighbor as yourself.' And he said to him, 'You have given the right answer: do this and you will live'" (Luke 10:25–28). Matthew and Mark both attribute the statement of the "two great commandments" to Jesus, while Luke puts them in the mouth of the lawyer, and then Luke relates that Jesus went on to tell the good Samaritan parable to illustrate what is meant by neighbor.

What is important about this teaching is not that it is something new, for it is not. The first part, about loving God, is in the sixth chapter of Deuteronomy (6:5), where it is part of a long explanation of the first commandment. The second part is found in the nineteenth chapter of Leviticus (19:17) and is part of what has become known as the "Holiness Code." The extension of this, the notion of taking care of foreigners, strangers, widows, and orphans is not new either, but appears in the twenty-second chapter of Exodus (22:21–24). Linking the two parts together amounts to a significant innovation, but the content of the teaching is solid, traditional wisdom. No, it is not new at all.

In the twenty-fifth chapter of Matthew's Gospel (25:40), Jesus links the love of God with the love of humanity and especially with the love of outcasts again, "as you did it to one of the least of these my brothers and sisters, you did it to me." There can be no love of God that does not express itself as love for others. Without love of God, the portrayal of love of others is nothing but a refined form of self-love. It is noteworthy that Jesus pares away all the dross and gets to the main point of what constitutes goodness in life. He came and preached a new way, a new way of relating to God together with a new way of relating to other people. Neither simpler nor easier in terms of practice, it is at least easier to put into words. Perhaps, because it is so simply articulated, it is far more difficult to practice, for the demands of personal responsibility and individual judgment are far greater and more complex. The traditional view taught that the law contained 613 precepts. By taking these 613 commandments and reducing them not to ten, as in the Decalogue, but to only two, he elevates the status of humanity; Jesus requires us to examine our motives and actions, to make decisions, and to take responsibility for our lives.

An important aspect of this is its optimism. By simplifying the statement of the law and by granting so very much autonomy and responsibility to human beings, the implication is that we are fundamentally good and capable of choosing to do good. Julian of Norwich, the first woman to write a book in English and who is noted for her overwhelming optimism, talked about the basic goodness of all that is made by God. She related that in a vision, granted to her in her thirtieth year, God showed her a little thing: the size of a hazelnut in the palm of her hand. She wondered what it might be, and the answer came, that "it is all that is made, and . . . it lasts and ever shall because God loves it."[1] She thought about that

---

1. Norwich, *Showings*, 183.

and reflected that all things have and maintain their being through the love of God. Elsewhere she wondered, in consequence, about the notion of sin, about the connection between being and activity. If God is in everything, God is the "first cause," nothing is done by chance, and God does not sin, then what are we? How did we come to exist? God is the light that drives away the darkness. God is the love that drives out fear. So, she concluded that sin is nothing, with no substance and no share in being. It seems that she identified sin as a thing in itself, a noun, and not a verb. Perhaps it can be both.

It is very easy to succumb to conventional views and to see ourselves (*pace* Bobby Burns) as others see us. Especially if those others see us as fundamentally sinful, shameful, and guilty of being what they are not. Those others could be well-meaning family, friends, coworkers, or neighbors, who have been hoodwinked into seeing spirituality and goodness as a matter of collecting trading stamps, or accumulating good works, or some other form of benign scrupulosity, masquerading as true religion. For too many of us, what we have heard from pulpit and hearthside is not this great teaching on love and compassion, but rather a flawed, human teaching both severe and judgmental, which almost cannot help but lead any of us to the darkness of despair. For far too many of us, we have been taught to link being and doing together so securely that a failure in activity is seen as reflective of a failure in being, doing something wrong implies an inherent, essential flaw in character, a fundamentally perverse and evil nature.

Yet, John the Beloved disciple, writing his first letter many years after the Gospels, reminds his friends, "This is the message you have heard from the beginning, that we should love one another" (1 John 3:11). A moment later, he says, "We know that we have passed from death to life, because we love one another" (3:14). Further on, he says, "Little children, let us love not in word or speech but in truth and action" (3:18). A little later, he returns to the same theme, saying, "Beloved, let us love one another, for love is from God; everyone who loves is born of God and knows God. Whoever does not love do not know God; for God is love. . . . So we have known and believe the love God has for us. God is love, and those who abide in love abide in God, and God abides in them" (4:7–8, 16).

Julian of Norwich, writing in the fourteenth century, echoes this teaching as she says, "I saw very surely that our substance is in God, and I also saw that God is in our sensuality, for in the same instant and place in which our soul is made sensual, in that same instant and place exists the city of God. . . . God is never out of the soul, in which [God] will dwell blessedly without end."[2]

Nothing in the party line, as expressed by these two divines, would lead us to think that there need be any essential or necessary connection between being and doing. Good acts do not necessarily demonstrate one's essential goodness. Their focus is on our inherent goodness grounded in our identities, in our connections with God. It is a matter of God expressed in and through us. For each of them, the matter of being godly is not a matter for discussion or disputation. It is self-evident and it is a reflection of God's love for us. The matter of behavior is a fit subject for consideration, but not on the same level as the matter of our being in God and God in us. Existence and activity are distinct, reflected in being and doing, essence and accident, one is inherent and the other transitory.

Close your eyes for a moment and think of your favorite teacher from high school or college. Call to mind what she or he looked like and wore and recall the sound of her or his voice. Now consider for a moment, do you happen by any chance to recall what exactly you learned? Do you remember any specific lesson as being far and away the best of the bunch of that year or semester? Do you recall a particularly brilliant demonstration of a principle or illustration of a concept? If you are like me, you probably do not. It turns out that I remember a number of instructors, brilliant teachers, who have influenced me in profound ways. But what I remember about them is their character, their personality, their love for students and for teaching. I remember their generosity, their sense of humor, and their soul. I remember them for who they were (and presumably are), rather for what they did or taught. Existence and activity are different indeed.

2. Norwich, *Showings*, 287.

Even Saint Paul, whom it is so easy and gratifying to vilify for his misogyny and heteropatriarchal sexism, in his letter to the Christians at Rome says that he does not understand his own actions, for he does what he does not want to do, and he neglects what he ought to do (Rom 7:15). It is probably to our advantage to pass over his unfortunate conclusion, that he (and everybody else) is fundamentally evil and sinful. Both good people and bad (according to our own subjective perceptions and evaluations) do what appear to us to be bad things and moreover, what appear to be bad things happen to those same people. Actions do not necessarily illustrate the condition of one's soul, and certainly have little necessary connection with character. When the action is being done, the person believes that s/he is doing good, on some level, and that the good which is being done somehow outweighs any evil that may arise. Even here there is an optimism about the essential nature of the individual soul, there is the sense that in truth, people are fundamentally good, and have good intentions. The matter then develops that what is necessary is to evolve personal capabilities to make decisions about actions. By the sixteenth century, one significant method of moral theology, at least in England, was casuistry, the technique of analysis of actions, of specific cases by type, in order to ensure by preparation that good decisions are likely to be made and that good is accomplished, not because good acts prove one's own goodness, but for their own sake, simply because they are good. Still, the focus was optimistic and focused on actions rather than identity.

By blurring the distinction between the activity and identity, it becomes very easy to confuse guilt with shame. Ronald and Patricia Potter-Efron point out that both of these are interpersonal emotions, both invite us to introspection and change, and both can be helpful in small doses but lethal when too strong.[3] Guilt points to a failure in action, while shame, which may be defined as a painful belief in one's fundamental defectiveness as a human being, concerns a failure in being. People afflicted with guilt are bothered by their transgressions and may fear punishment, while

3. Potter-Efron and Potter-Efron, *Shame*.

those afflicted by shame are distressed by their personal shortcomings, and fear abandonment as a consequence of their inadequacy. Guilt may cripple, but shame can kill.

The Potter-Efrons suggest that shame is significantly a spiritual crisis, the individual feels less than human, feels that s/he is a mistake, a shame, not just ashamed. There is often a feeling of isolation (from other people as well as from God), of worthlessness, and of emptiness. Too, there is sometimes an appearance of arrogance and an affectation of rage, which serve very effectively to cover the sense of internal emptiness, nothingness, and bankruptcy. Continually aware of their defects, shame-based people often think that even trivial mistakes prove their inadequacy and that failures are permanent, while accomplishments are transitory. For far too many of us, we still admit to others, to ourselves, and to God that we are trans folk. Too many of us see this as a failure of being, and we are plunged into a serious spiritual crisis and the darkness of despair. When shame remains, in time it becomes gangrenous and contaminates and infects the soul. The awareness of goodness within disappears and the shame itself turns into self-hatred, disgust, and contempt.

Jesus keeps the focus steady here: the question is "what must I do" to inherit life, it is not "what should I be" or "who should I be." It is assumed that we are fundamentally good and fundamentally capable of making decisions about our lives and actions in such a way as to reflect that fundamental goodness. No longer is it a matter of unhesitating observance of the letter of the law in every detail, no longer is it a matter of doubting or denying our own essential goodness, no longer is it a matter of not trusting ourselves (poor, weak sinners) to do right. Rather it is up to each one of us to take responsibility for our actions, for our thoughts and words, for the consequences of our behavior. Thomas and Patricia Potter-Efron point out that it is of major importance in overcoming shame to keep in mind several key principles, that we are all uncompromisingly, indisputably human, and that we are all essentially equal, autonomous, and competent. It is the same fundamentally optimistic perspective shared by Jesus, Saint John, and Julian of Norwich. Out of these notions, then, we may find suddenly that intent may sometimes be more important than action. Suddenly motivation is a factor, an attitude, and the thoughts of our hearts are matters for meditation. Suddenly we are removed from a law based in severity and mercy, and we are immersed in a new way of life, based in a politics of compassion, centered in a recognition and appreciation of our common humanity. A politics of compassion? Politics again? Well, let us go back and look at Luke's version of what happened.

Asked by the lawyer, "And who is my neighbor?" Jesus tells the parable of the good Samaritan (Luke 10:25–37). What is very interesting here is that some twenty years before, about the time that Jesus was presented in the temple at the age of twelve, that very temple was defiled during the Passover feast by someone introducing human remains into it. It was said that the deed had been done by a group of Samaritans and the Samaritans were even more fiercely hated ever since.[4] Imagine how difficult it must have been for the lawyer to see or admit that it was the Samaritan who was neighbor to the injured man. Imagine how difficult it must have been for the crowd to see anything good about a Samaritan. In the desecration of the temple, actions had been blurred into identity, and by their very existence the Samaritans began to be seen as shameful, as sinful. Now in this parable, Jesus blurs the distinction between enemy and friend, enemy and neighbor, enemy and deliverer. The distinctions were blurred, not only for those hearing the parable, but even within the parable itself. The victim who was touched and saved by what might have seemed to be an unclean and evil outcast may have reacted with horror and disgust. The innkeeper faced with the prospect of having a business transaction with that same evil sinner, faced with the prospect of staining his home with the victim's blood, and faced with the obligation to act with compassion, might have recoiled in horror, just as did the priest and the Levite. The Samaritan, too, was faced with the dubious opportunity of demonstrating compassion, of saving one

4. "Samaritan."

of the very people that hated him with an intensity that could not be expressed. Enemy or victim? Enemy or neighbor?

Outsiders and insiders. In the time of Jesus of Nazareth, it was not uncommon for the enthusiastic and educated students of the Law to look down on the unlettered peasants whose entire lives were consumed in living through one day and surviving until the next. The educated ones tended often to see themselves as holier, as more beloved of God, as true Israelites living in faultless conformity with the law. By contrast, the peasants, the *am ha'aretz*, had little regard for the nuances of the Torah, and were content, it seemed, to live their lives as best they were able. The *am ha'aretz* were hated and despised by the observant and scholarly Pharisees.

Now here we are. Who are our Samaritans? Who are our *am ha'aretz*? Too often, I am afraid, it seems we LGBTQ people are. We hate ourselves almost as much as the outside world seems to hate us. We oppress and exclude ourselves from groups, from churches, and from social and service organizations. We draw imaginary distinctions among ourselves and then exclude some of us from the rest of us. (The eminent twentieth-century philosopher-comic Groucho Marx spoke for many of us when he said once that he would never lower himself to join any club that would admit him as a member.) We thus fail to exercise the duties and obligations of our citizenship, of our humanity, to defend ourselves and others who are oppressed by cultural, ethnic, or religious groups who would ostracize and exclude us from full citizenship and from the love of God.

Here is one more twist on identity politics: can one of those people whose very humanity is subject to dispute—whose identity has been regarded as inherently shameful, even inherently sinful—can one of those people possibly be fundamentally good? Can one of those people do greater good than one of us people? Imagine how difficult it was for that lawyer, or for anyone who remembered the scandal of twenty years earlier, to see that love of neighbor involves reconciliation with all those whom God loves, quite aside from political, cultural, or religious matters. These commandments to love, especially that to love our neighbors, are tremendously important, in part because they involve us in the work of God—to love and contribute to the reconciliation of the universe.

Participation through love in this way, in the work of God, is certainly not unique to Christianity. Isaac Luria was a disciple of Moses Cordovero, of the great intellectual center at Safed. A key aspect of the Lurianic school of Kabbalists, dating from the sixteenth century of the Common Era, is the more-than-a-little complex doctrine of the *tikkun,* of the reconciliation and redemption of the universe. A very small aspect of his teaching is that through both internal and external works, through prayer and the fulfillment of the commandments, through maturity in good thoughts and good works, through every act, one hastens the coming of the Messiah and the return of the *Shekhinah* from exile, and one contributes to the restoration of the original unity, integrity, and simplicity of primordial creation. Note the focus: Luria finds that the redemption and restoration of the world lies in personal acts of responsible individuals, not in individual identities. What is critical is that we are called to holiness of life and of activity.[5]

Four centuries later, the theme is still strong. There are some who expect the arrival of *moshiach,* the messiah, in this very generation. Indeed, the late beloved Reb Menachem Schneersohn, the Lubavitcher Rebbe, taught that the way to prepare for the arrival of *moschiach* is by "acts of goodness and kindliness." Again, we are called to personal action, not to any specific kind of personal identity. Our lives and the very life of the world are certainly to be transformed, redeemed, and restored, not by any kind of twisting or forced conformity of identities, but rather by action. Action that may range from the heroic to the commonplace, action which reflects what we understand to be the best of which we are capable.

Innovation, especially among theologians and divines, is often resisted, and so it is not surprising that this clarification and development of the idea of ethical behavior was not greeted with universal joyful assent when articulated by Jesus and his followers. More often than not, theological innovation is seen as heresy—it

5. Scholem, *Mysticism,* 217.

drives nervous people ever closer and closer to the orthodox party line and strengthens their resolve and resistance. Indeed, even among Jesus's followers, among whose spiritual descendants must include those who constitute the so-called Christian right, it happened that additional rules, footnotes, and explanations began to be enunciated. Although medieval Christian theologians defined scrupulosity as a serious impediment to spirituality and they discovered it to have great potential for leading one into sin, that has not prevented a great many of our fellow citizens from using that profoundly counterproductive mental exercise to mask their own shame, to express their rage, and to inflict pain and suffering on others.

Jesus does not call or expect us to admit guilt for being who we are, for indeed we are created in the image and likeness of God. He does not intimate that we should capitulate to shame and disgrace for being the perfect creatures, the perfect children of an infinitely creative, loving God. Jesus does not call us to renounce our identities, to hide, or to deny ourselves, for what shame could possibly be associated with being a trans person? Jesus calls us to a new way of living, a way based in personal responsibility, in spiritual adulthood, based in the love of God and of one another, and based in genuine acceptance and love of ourselves as we are.

At the end of his letter to the Galatians, Paul reminded them that what really matters is not that someone conforms to the letter of the law, but that s/he is an adopted child of God, and so is, effectively, a new creation (Gal 6:15). He calls them (and us) to reexamine our motivations for doing what we do, for although good works are laudable, we must not mistake them for indicators of character, godliness, or goodness. He calls us to take honest and realistic responsibility for our actions and to build that strength of character on the rock of our fundamental divinity, of our dynamic participation in the divinity of the God who fashioned us and loves us.

16

Zeal, Inclusion, and Unity

ON MY DESK I have a small piece of cement. It may not seem like much, but this little rock is a piece of history. It is a piece of hatred and a reminder of how people can lose sight of their shared humanity. And it is also a symbol of revolution and optimism. This is a piece of the Berlin Wall, which came down on November 9, 1989.

More than forty years ago, U.S. President John F. Kennedy stood in front of that wall, in front of the Brandenburg Gate, and identified himself and all Americans with the anguish and injustice of separation, of segregation, saying, "I am a Berliner."[1] Twenty years ago, in a made-for-television moment, Ronald Reagan said, "Mr. Gorbachev, tear down this wall."[2] And so they did.

As a piece of that wall, this rock is a visual reminder of other walls—around the Warsaw Ghetto, Palestine, the Great Wall of China, Hadrian's Wall, the Wall of Apartheid, and the Iron Curtain of the Cold War era. The iconostasis in the Christian East or the communion rail in the West. The walls of racism, classism, sexism, homophobia, and transphobia. They keep out, or they keep in, those who seem to be outsiders. They divide families, people,

---

1. "Ich Bin ein Berliner."
2. "President Reagan Challenges Gorbachev."

and nations, and they infect us and our institutions with hatred, fear, injustice, and oppression. Their destruction, then, is a revolutionary act, to destroy the Berlin Wall in 1989, to do something revolutionary, and to inaugurate something new.

Revolution. Tearing down walls, opening windows, dissolving differences in the cause of truth, is at the root of what we do in our church building and communities of faith. In Christ there is neither slave nor free, male nor female, Jew nor Greek; all of us are one in Christ (Gal 3:28). Indeed, we are called to be revolutionaries, to seek to serve one another as equals, without borders, barriers, or walls. Moreover, we are called to serve and to care for the earth, to be that living water that nourishes every sort of living creature, fish, and fruit tree.

Today God calls us to look again at our church and our communities, to see if we are truly inclusive, if we are truly united. The Defenders, the Catholic leather/Levi group, founded in 1981, recognized five significant attributes of the human person: emotional, psychological, physical, sexual, and spiritual. They call us to nurture each of these aspects. Moreover, they call us to widen the reach of our tent to promote acceptance and celebration of the leather community as full and equal members of the body of Christ.

Saint John's Gospel account of the cleansing of the Jerusalem temple (John 2:13-22) differs from the Synoptics in that he tells us that Jesus uses a whip to drive out the merchants and in that he does this cleansing at the beginning of his ministry, right after the wedding feast at Cana. It is another epiphany moment, another revelation of Christ's radical divinity. Here was this nobody, with no credentials, no connections, no education to speak of, turning that little corner of the world upside down—with a whip. His followers were the *anawim*, the notoriously ignorant sinners of the very lowest classes, illiterate peasants and fishermen, tax collectors, and *women*, for heaven's sake! All the sorts of people who belonged, and rightfully, so they said, outside the walls of the Jerusalem temple, outside the walls of polite society, and outside the walls of God's commonwealth. The religious establishment had their traditions, their ways of doing business, and they were not about to change things. They were filled with zeal, with commitment, with the maintaining of the status quo. Certainly, they were not about to change things just because some nobody with a handful of illiterate nobody friends told them they should. In light of the impossibility of reasoning with them, they got angry and made the changes anyway.

"Zeal for your house will consume me" (John 2:17). The walls of our homes and our church buildings need to be seen as permeable, with gates and portals from which may flow those streams of living water. The walls must be not walls of separation, of division, and of alienation, but of inclusion. Moreover, these walls certainly cannot contain God, who is ever a God of surprises. And we may find the voice of God in unexpected places; for God's revelation to us continues to move in the lives of those who are able to listen.

If we are, as we say, members of the mystical body of Christ, we must affirm the surpassing goodness of that house. The church still struggles with the dualism of the early gnostics, who saw matter and the body as somehow inherently evil. We, too, struggle with anxiety and guilt when it comes to the enjoyment of our bodies and our sexuality or sexualities. Part of the beauty and wonder of the LGBTQ communities is that we affirm and celebrate the goodness of our bodies as well as our souls and spirits, and what is more, we see all this as a source of grace and redemption.

What this means for us today is that we must recognize our obligation to discipleship, to think and to discern the truth, to the best of our abilities, and to resist untruth in all its forms. Discipleship is not membership in a social club, but it is an attitude of mind, a quality of soul, and a way of living that has serious political implications. We are the very members incorporate of the mystery of Christ's body and blood, all of us constituting the temple of God, the mystical body of Christ. We are called to conscious inclusion and to public advocacy for change.

It seems that God continues to speak to us if we would only listen. In this connection, a number of years ago members of the Women's Ordination Conference identified three ministries, three ways of responding to official oppression. They identified the ministry of patience in prayer, of irritation, and of service. There are those among us who are called to prayer and patient witness—*It's my Church and I'll Stay if I Want To* is the title of a recent book by Lonnie Collins Pratt, and it makes very specific some aspects of the ministry of patience.[3] There are those likewise who feel called to prophecy—to irritate the hierarchy, to press for change, to call for action, and to tell them the truth in season and out of season. There are those who move ahead, without support from the hierarchy, to engage in the work that must be done, under the aegis of autonomous organizations, independent bishops, or other denominations.

God calls us all to zeal, then. Zeal for the house of God, zeal for the human community, zeal for one another, and zeal for equality in an inclusive and loving church and in our nation and its laws. In the fifth century, St. Benedict characterized a good zeal that separates from evil and leads to God and everlasting life: "To love and support one another, and to prefer nothing whatever to Christ. And may He bring us all together to everlasting life."[4] Amen!

3. Pratt, *Church.*
4. Benedict, *Rule,* 295.

Bibliography

Adler, Mortimer J. *How to Think about God: A Guide for the 20th-Century Pagan*. New York: Touchstone, 1991.

Augustine, Saint. "Our Hearts are Restless." Christian History Institute, n.d. https://christianhistoryinstitute.org/incontext/article/augustine.

Benedict, Saint. *RB 80: The Rule of St. Benedict in Latin and English with Notes*. Collegeville, MN: Liturgical, 1980.

Blaine, Rick. "I'm No Good at Being Noble." Goodreads, n.d. https://www.goodreads.com/quotes/34321-i-m-no-good-at-being-noble-but-it-doesn-t-take.

Boswell, John. *Same-Sex Unions in Premodern Europe*. New York: Vintage, 1995.

Cannon, Justin. *Homosexuality in the Orthodox Church*. Self-published, gayorthodox.com, 2011.

Cheng, Patrick S. *Radical Love: An Introduction to Queer Theology*. New York: Seabury, 2011.

Cleaver, Richard. *Know My Name: A Gay Liberation Theology*. Louisville: Westminster John Knox Press, 1995.

Denny, Dallas, ed. *Current Concepts in Transgender Identity*. New York: Garland, 1998.

Doherty, Catherine. "Our Little Mandate." Madonna House, n.d. https://www.madonnahouse.org/.

—————. *Poustinia: Encountering God in Silence, Solitude, and Prayer*. Combermere, ON: Madonna House, 2000.

Durka, Gloria. *Praying with Hildegard of Bingen*. Companions for the Journey Series. Frederick, MD: Word Among Us, 1991.

Eco, Umberto. *The Name of the Rose*. New York: Harcourt Brace & Co., 1983.

"The Epistle of Mathetes to Diognetus." In *Ante-Nicene Fathers*, edited by Alexander Roberts et al., translated by Alexander Roberts and James Donaldson, vol. 1. Buffalo: Christian Literature Publishing, 1885. Rev. and ed. by Kevin Knight. https://www.newadvent.org/fathers/0101.htm.

Feldman, Deborah. *Exodus: A Memoir*. New York: Plume, 2014.

———. *Unorthodox: The Scandalous Rejection of My Hasidic Roots.* New York: Simon and Schuster, 2012.

Girzone, Joseph. *Joshua: A Parable for Today.* New York: Touchstone, 1995.

Goethe, Johann Wolfgang von. "Life Is the Childhood of Our Immortality." Brainy Quote, n.d. https://www.brainyquote.com/quotes/johann_wolfgang_von_goeth_118416.

Hildegard, Saint. "Meditation: Hildegard of Bingen." The Christian Masters, Apr 12, 2023. https://chippit.tripod.com/hildegard.html.

Homan, Daniel, and Lonni Collins Pratt. *Radical Hospitality: Benedict's Way of Love.* Brewster, MA: Paraclete, 2002.

"Ich Bin ein Berliner." Wikipedia, n.d. https://en.wikipedia.org/wiki/Ich_bin_ein_Berliner.

Norwich, Julian of. *Showings.* Translated by Edmund Colledge and James Walsh. Ramsey, NJ: Paulist, 1978.

Ladin, Joy. *Through the Door of Life: A Jewish Journey between Genders.* Madison: University of Wisconsin Press, 2012.

Lawrence, T. E. *Seven Pillars of Wisdom.* New York: Anchor Books, 1991.

Lewis, C. S. *Mere Christianity.* New York: Touchstone Books, 1999.

Mandeville, John. *Travels of Sir John Mandeville.* Salt Lake City: Project Gutenberg, 2014. https://www.gutenberg.org/files/782/782-h/782-h.htm.

Merton, Thomas. *The Wisdom of the Desert.* New York: New Directions, 1960.

Mollenkott, Virginia Ramey, and Vanessa Sheridan. *Transgender Journeys.* Eugene, OR: Resource, 2003.

Moore, Thomas. *Care of the Soul: A Guide for Cultivating Depth and Sacredness in Everyday Life.* New York: HarperCollins, 1994.

Morris, Stephen. *"When Brothers Dwell in Unity": Byzantine Christianity and Homosexuality.* Jefferson, NC: McFarland & Company, 2016.

Parker, Ian. "The Gift." *New Yorker,* Jul 25, 2005. https://www.newyorker.com/magazine/2004/08/02/the-gift-ian-parker.

Peck, M. Scott. *The Different Drum: Community Making and Peace.* New York: Touchstone, 1998.

Peguy, Charles. *Basic Verities: Poetry & Prose.* Providence, RI: Cluny Media, 2019.

pmarkrobb [username]. "A Permanent Mark." Journey OnWord, Aug 11, 2013. https://journeyonword.com/2013/08/11/a-permanent-mark-2/.

Potter-Efron, Ronald T., and Patricia S. Potter-Efron. *Letting Go of Shame: Understanding How Shame Affects Your Life.* Center City, MN: Hazelden, 1989.

Pratt, Lonnie Collins. *It's My Church and I'll Stay if I Want To.* Chicago: Triumph Books, 2003.

"President Reagan Challenges Gorbachev to 'Tear Down This Wall.'" History, Jun 5, 2023. https://www.history.com/this-day-in-history/reagan-challenges-gorbachev-to-tear-down-the-berlin-wall.

"Samaritan." McClintock and Strong Biblical Cyclopedia, n.d. https://www.biblicalcyclopedia.com/S/samaritan.html.

Scholem, Gershon. *Major Trends in Jewish Mysticism.* New York: Schocken, 1995.

———, ed. *Zohar: The Book of Splendor; Basic Readings from the Kabbalah.* New York: Schocken, 1995.

Spong, John Shelby. *This Hebrew Lord.* New York: HarperCollins, 1993.

Stein, Abby Chava. *Becoming Eve: My Journey from Ultra-Orthodox Rabbi to Transgender Woman.* New York: Seal Press, 2019.

Tannehill, Brynn. *Everything You Ever Wanted to Know about Trans (But Were Afraid to Ask).* Philadelphia: Jessica Kingsley, 2019.

Tannen, Deborah. *You Just Don't Understand: Women and Men in Conversation.* New York: Quill, 1990.

"Transgender Day of Remembrance." GLAAD, n.d. https://glaad.org/tdor/.

Weekley, David E. *In from the Wilderness: Sherman; She-r-man.* Eugene, OR: Wipf & Stock, 2011.

Wilchins, Riki Anne. *Read My Lips: Sexual Subversion and the End of Gender.* Ithaca, NY: Firebrand, 2005.

"William of Ockham's Nominalism." Philo-Notes, Apr 21, 2023. https://philonotes.com/2023/04/william-of-ockhams-nominalism.

Williams, Robert. *Just as I Am: A Practical Guide to Being Out, Proud and Christian.* New York: Harper Perennial, 1992.

Woolf, Virginia. *Three Guineas.* Boston: Mariner Books Classics, 1963.